NEW DIRECTIONS FOR CHILD DEVELOPMENT

William Damon, *Brown University*
EDITOR-IN-CHIEF

Economic Stress: Effects on Family Life and Child Development

Vonnie C. McLoyd
University of Michigan

Constance A. Flanagan
University of Michigan

EDITORS

Number 46, Winter 1990

JOSSEY-BASS INC., PUBLISHERS
San Francisco • Oxford

Economic Stress: Effects on Family Life and Child Development.
Vonnie C. McLoyd, Constance A. Flanagan (eds.).
New Directions for Child Development, no. 46.

NEW DIRECTIONS FOR CHILD DEVELOPMENT
William Damon, Editor-in-Chief

Copyright © 1990 by Jossey-Bass Inc., Publishers
and
Jossey-Bass Limited

Copyright under International, Pan American, and Universal Copyright Conventions. All rights reserved. No part of this issue may be reproduced in any form—except for a brief quotation (not to exceed 500 words) in a review or professional work—without permission in writing from the publishers.

NEW DIRECTIONS FOR CHILD DEVELOPMENT is part of The Jossey-Bass Social and Behavioral Science Series and is published quarterly by Jossey-Bass Inc., Publishers (publication number USPS 494-090). Second-class postage paid at San Francisco, California, and at additional mailing offices. Postmaster: Send address changes to Jossey-Bass Inc., Publishers, 350 Sansome Street, San Francisco, California 94104.

EDITORIAL CORRESPONDENCE should be sent to the Editor-in-Chief, William Damon, Department of Education, Box 1938, Brown University, Providence, Rhode Island 02912.

Library of Congress Catalog Card Number LC 85-644581
International Standard Serial Number ISSN 0195-2269
International Standard Book Number ISBN 1-55542-845-2

Cover photograph by Wernher Krutein/PHOTOVAULT.
Manufactured in the United States of America. Printed on acid-free paper.

Contents

EDITORS' NOTES 1
Vonnie C. McLoyd, Constance A. Flanagan

1. Families and Schools in Hard Times 7
Constance A. Flanagan
Economic recessions affect children by conditioning their aspirations, straining parent-child relations, and limiting educational quality.

2. Family Income Loss and Economic Hardship: Antecedents 27
of Adolescents' Problem Behavior
Rainer K. Silbereisen, Sabine Walper, Helfried T. Albrecht
Income loss leads to lower family integration, which in turn makes adolescents more sensitive to evaluation by peers. This can result in lower self-esteem and an inclination to act against common rules and norms.

3. Maternal Behavior, Social Support, and Economic Conditions 49
as Predictors of Distress in Children
Vonnie C. McLoyd, Leon Wilson
Economic hardship diminishes psychological well-being and the capacity for supportive parenting. Single mothers' coping behavior, psychological functioning, and communications to the child about financial matters and personal problems predict the degree of psychological distress experienced by their children.

4. The Iowa Farm Crisis: Perceptions, Interpretations, 71
and Family Patterns
Mary P. Van Hook
Economic changes in the Farm Belt have undermined the security of life on the family farm. Rural adolescents are trying to come to terms with the meaning of the "farm crisis" for their identity and for their future.

5. The Adolescent-to-Adult Transition: Discouragement Among 87
Jobless Black Youth
Phillip J. Bowman
Because of chronic joblessness, the adolescent-to-adult transition is a special psycho-social challenge for black youth, with far-reaching developmental implications.

6. The Development of Concepts of Economic 107
and Social Inequality
Robert L. Leahy
With increasing age, children explain wealth and poverty by referring to individual differences in work, effort, and intelligence rather than social-structural or political factors. Such explanations of inequality support a belief in a just world where the "losers" are viewed as obtaining their just due.

INDEX 121

Editors' Notes

The decade of the 1980s was marked by rising rates of unemployment among adults, higher rates of poverty among children, and increased inequity in income. Back-to-back recessions in 1980 and 1981–1982, combined with retrenchments and changes in production methods in major manufacturing industries in response to foreign competition, resulted in an unemployment rate of 10.6 percent in late 1982, the highest since the Great Depression of the 1930s. Poverty rates among American children soared during the 1980s. Between 1959 and 1969, the rate declined sharply from 26 percent to 14 percent, followed by a slight rise throughout the 1970s and a sharp increase between 1979 and 1984, leveling off at roughly 22 percent (Halpern, 1987). During the past two decades, families with the fewest economic resources suffered the most, while the economic well-being of those in the highest income brackets actually improved. Families in the bottom one-fifth of the 1986 income distribution had adjusted incomes that were only 88 percent of what their counterparts received in 1970, whereas families in the top one-fifth had adjusted incomes that were 127 percent higher in 1986 than 1970 (Duncan, 1988).

Despite its affluence, the United States is distinguished among Western industrialized countries by the extent of economic privation among its children. During the 1980s, the United States had the highest proportion of children living in poverty (in 1984, one of every five American children under age eighteen lived in poverty) and was the only industrialized country in which children constituted the largest age group living in poverty (in 1985, 38 percent of all the poor were children) (Children's Defense Fund, 1984; Duncan, 1988).

A substantial number of America's children have also experienced a significant decline in their standard of living. This is clearly documented by the Panel Study of Income Dynamics (PSID), a longitudinal study conducted at the University of Michigan that has charted the economic well-being of a nationally representative sample of American families each year since 1968. More than one-quarter (27 percent) of all children in this study lived in households in which the income-to-needs ratio fell by more than 50 percent at least once between 1969 and 1979, and this economic decline pushed more than one-third of the families into poverty. A major spell of unemployment was the most frequent labor market event preceding economic decline, followed by reductions in work hours due to illness of the family head. Divorce or separation was the most frequent family composition event precipitating economic decline. Compared to families in general, families with children were less likely to have anticipated the losses and to have savings available to buffer the impact of the largely unforeseen event. Consequently, they probably experienced an exacerbation of the difficulties occasioned by sharp income loss (Duncan, 1988).

A disproportionate share of the burden of poverty and economic decline is borne by black families. Poverty among black children is marked by its persistence and geographic concentration, whereas it is primarily a transitory, geographically diffuse phenomenon among white children (Duncan and Rodgers, 1988; Wilson, 1987). In the PSID, for example, black children accounted for the total number of children who were consistently poor during a selected fifteen-year period and for almost 90 percent of the children who were poor during at least ten of fifteen years. Because they are not well-off to begin with, black children are more likely than white children to fall into poverty after events that reduce economic resources (divorce, job loss, cutbacks in work hours). In the last two decades, low wages, increasing levels of black male unemployment, and, relatedly, the rise and duration of stay in female-headed households have combined to threaten the economic well-being of black children even more than in earlier times (Center for the Study of Social Policy, 1986; Edelman, 1987; Wilson, 1987).

These trends have focused the concern of social scientists on the effects of economic change and adversity on children's development. This volume of *New Directions for Child Development* was motivated by the alarming decline in children's economic well-being and reports findings from recent efforts to understand the effects of this decline. These efforts in particular, and the fields of developmental psychology, human development, and sociology in general, owe a great debt to Glen Elder and his colleagues for drawing attention to the implications of economic change for development and for identifying some of the mechanisms by which economic decline alters the lives of children and their parents. Their research on families of the Great Depression stands as an impressive person-process-context model that has motivated efforts to understand similar issues in the contemporary context.

Five of the six chapters in this volume summarize findings from investigations of the effects of economic hardship and decline. While these investigations vary widely in scale, represent different methodologies, and focus on groups that differ in cultural background, racial group membership, social class, and nationality, each is concerned with the mechanisms by which economic hardship influences the psychological functioning, behavior, and life chances of children and adolescents.

Constance A. Flanagan argues in Chapter One that economic recessions affect objective conditions and socialization processes in families and schools. She presents cross-sectional and longitudinal data from the Transitions in Early Adolescence Project, a two-year study conducted during the recession of the 1980s. Using cross-sectional data she relates differences in adolescents' aspirations to changes in their parents' work status and argues that such changes affect parents' roles as achievement models in subtle ways. Using the longitudinal component of the study, Flanagan concludes that hardship compromises parents' ability to respond to their adolescents' developmental needs and that reemployment compensates for initial tensions in parent–adolescent authority relations. Finally, she uses qualitative data from teachers and principals to support the thesis that recessions impede the ability of schools to equalize opportunities for all students.

In Chapter Two, Rainer K. Silbereisen, Sabine Walper, and Helfried T. Albrecht report findings from their cross-sectional and longitudinal studies of the effects of income loss on West German parents and children. Their research is part of the Berlin Youth Longitudinal Study, an ongoing study of personality development in adolescence and young adulthood. Silbereisen and his colleagues are able to test different models of mediation and causality because they gathered repeated assessments of these families over time. Among the particularly important insights provided by their work is that income loss leads to lower family integration (as perceived by fathers) by increasing parental strains and the mother's decision-making power. Among less educated families, declines in family integration brought on by economic loss result in a decrease in adolescents' self-esteem and, in turn, an increase in their inclination to act against rules and norms.

In Chapter Three, Vonnie C. McLoyd and Leon Wilson report findings from a study of black and nonblack single mothers and their children, many of whom received Aid to Families with Dependent Children. This research adds to the growing body of evidence that economic hardship threatens the psychological well-being of parents and undermines their capacity for supportive child rearing. McLoyd and Wilson's findings suggest that the mother's psychological functioning and her patterns of communication have important implications for the degree of psychological distress experienced by the child. By identifying factors that explain variation in psychological well-being, this study underscores the heterogeneity of economically deprived individuals.

In Chapter Four, Mary P. Van Hook presents the results of a qualitative study of the farm crisis and its meaning for rural adolescents and their families. She contends that the strengths of rural families not only see them through hard times but also intensify the burden of responsibility felt by adolescents. The farm crisis has reduced the attractiveness of farming as an occupation and has undermined the legacy that Iowa farmers have traditionally passed on to their children.

Chronic joblessness is a major problem for black youth making the transition from adolescence to adulthood. In Chapter Five, Phillip J. Bowman takes a life-span approach and argues that job discouragement among black youth undermines their ability to meet role expectations at later stages of the life cycle. He contends that cultural resources may facilitate adaptive responses to job search strains, but public policy initiatives are ultimately needed to reduce the structural barriers to black youth employment. Bowman's analysis of the rippling effects of youth unemployment on later development is consistent with data from the National Longitudinal Survey of Youth Labor Market Experience. These data suggest that labor market experience during high school is conducive to subsequent labor market success in black adolescents who do not attend college (for example, higher hourly wages, fewer weeks of unemployment). High school employment may reduce later unemployment partly because a substantial percentage of youth continue in the jobs they hold as students or use their high school jobs as a source of information about related job opportunities (D'Amico and Baker, 1984).

Explanations for economic inequality are important, in part, because they guide behavior. The prevailing view in American society is that poverty is a consequence of individual deficiencies. If this view results in disdainful behavior toward the poor, intensifies feelings of self-blame among the poor, and contributes to the rising incidence of poverty in this country, and we believe that it does, the findings reported by Robert L. Leahy in Chapter Six are disheartening. His work shows that with increasing age, both black and white children (and children of all social classes) increasingly legitimize economic inequality by reference to individual differences in effort, ability, intelligence, and personality. In short, children internalize a victim-blaming perspective as they develop. The children and adolescents studied by Leahy gave little credence to social-structural or political factors as contributors to vast economic disparities. Leahy argues that equity explanations of inequality support a belief in a just world where the "losers" are viewed as obtaining their just due.

Drastic cutbacks in social programs for the poor, the demise of job training programs, failure to increase the minimum wage (which has been held at the same level since January 1981 despite rising inflation), retrenchments in affirmative action programs, and changes in the tax structure, in large part, are responsible for the increase in poverty during the decade of the 1980s. These changes have intensified race and class cleavages in American society. Social policies at the local, state, and federal level are needed to reverse these trends. Displacement of workers is expected to continue as the manufacturing sector of the economy declines. In addition, fewer companies in the rapidly growing service sector are expected to provide lifetime employment because they will be smaller and have higher turnover rates. These projections suggest that work life will be characterized by more frequent changes in salary, employers, and occupations. Policies are needed to ensure that these transitions will cause a minimum of stress to workers and their families. We hope that the research presented in this volume will inform and contribute to such policy formation.

During the preparation of this volume, Vonnie C. McLoyd was supported by a Faculty Scholar Award from the William T. Grant Foundation. Constance Flanagan was awarded research release time by Provost Eugene Arden of the University of Michigan-Dearborn's Office of Academic Affairs. We gratefully acknowledge their support and the editorial assistance of Eve Trager and Audrey Tran at the Center for Human Growth and Development, University of Michigan-Ann Arbor. The opinions expressed in this volume are those of the authors and do not necessarily reflect the views of any of the institutions and agencies that provided support.

Vonnie C. McLoyd
Constance A. Flanagan
Editors

References

Center for the Study of Social Policy. "The 'Flip-Side' of Black Families Headed by Women: The Economic Status of Black Men." In R. Staples (ed.), *The Black Family: Essays and Studies.* Belmont, Calif.: Wadsworth, 1986.

Children's Defense Fund. *American Children in Poverty.* Washington, D.C.: Children's Defense Fund, 1984.

D'Amico, R., and Baker, P. "The Nature and Consequence of High School Employment." In P. Baker, S. Carpenter, J. Crowley, R. D'Amico, C. Kim, W. Morgan, and J. Wielgosz (eds.), *Pathways to the Future: A Report on the National Longitudinal Surveys of Youth Labor Market Experience.* Vol. 4. Columbus: Ohio State University Center for Human Resource Research, 1984.

Duncan, G. "The Economic Environment of Childhood." Paper presented at a study group meeting on poverty and children, University of Kansas, Lawrence, June 1988.

Duncan, G., and Rodgers, W. "Longitudinal Aspects of Childhood Poverty." *Journal of Marriage and the Family,* 1988, 50, 1007-1021.

Edelman, M. W. *Families in Peril: An Agenda for Social Change.* Cambridge, Mass.: Harvard University Press, 1987.

Halpern, R. "Major Social and Demographic Trends Affecting Young Families: Implications for Early Childhood Care and Education." *Young Children,* 1987, 42, 34-40.

Wilson, W. J. *The Truly Disadvantaged: The Inner City, the Underclass, and Public Policy.* Chicago: University of Chicago Press, 1987.

Vonnie C. McLoyd is associate professor in the Department of Psychology and research associate in the Center for Human Growth and Development at the University of Michigan. She is the principal investigator of a longitudinal study of the impact of maternal job and income loss on African American children and their families, funded by the National Institute of Mental Health.

Constance A. Flanagan is an assistant professor of psychology at the University of Michigan–Dearborn, where she directs the Women's Studies Program.

Economic recessions affect children by conditioning their aspirations, straining parent-child relations, and limiting educational quality.

Families and Schools in Hard Times

Constance A. Flanagan

Structural change in the American economy has disrupted communities and caused a steady erosion of the standard of living of many American families (Harrison and Bluestone, 1988). An increasing awareness among social scientists that work and family life are interdependent systems and that change in one setting disrupts life in the other has focused attention on the social costs of economic change. Research has shown that unemployment has deleterious effects on the mental and physical health of workers and their spouses (Dew, Bromet, and Schulberg, 1987; Kessler, Turner, and House, 1989; Liem and Liem, 1989).

Parallel to the work on adults is a growing body of empirical evidence that a changing economy also has an impact on children. Since statistics maintained by the Department of Labor do not provide information about the parental status of the unemployed, we do not have good estimates of the numbers of children that may be affected by paren-

---

The preparation of this chapter was supported in part by a Research Release Time Award, for which I would like to thank Provost Eugene Arden of the University of Michigan–Dearborn. I would like to thank Jacquelynne Eccles for allowing me to append a study of economic change to her study of early adolescent transitions. The Transitions at Early Adolescence Study was made possible by grants from the National Institute of Mental Health (MH31724), the National Institute of Child Health and Human Development (HD17296), and the William T. Grant Foundation (83-0917-00) to Jacquelynne Eccles. The assistance of my colleagues at the Achievement Research Laboratory in collecting and processing these data is gratefully acknowledged. Portions of this research were presented in an invited symposium at the biennial meeting of the International Society for the Study of Behavioral Development, Jyväskylä, Finland, July 1989.

tal job loss. We do know that low-seniority workers with young families are a high-risk group for layoffs (Moen, 1983) and can assume that, as dependents, children are affected when their parents are coping with dislocations on the job.

In this chapter I discuss three ways in which a changing economy affects the settings of childhood and the course of children's development. First, the psychological costs borne by unemployed or demoted parents can affect their role as achievement models for children. The socialization of children's achievement aspirations depends on these modeling processes as well as on the very real restrictions that financial hardship imposes. When income declines, families accommodate by cutting back, an act that may limit a child's opportunities and condition her or his future aspirations. As Moen, Kain, and Elder (1983) argue, what is functional for the family in the short run may have inadvertent but significant consequences for children's life prospects. Second, when parents are coping with a lack of job security or income loss they are preoccupied with issues of family welfare. Responsive parenting is minimized under such conditions, and parents are less patient and nurturant with their children and adolescents (Harold, Radin, and Eccles, 1988; Lempers, Clark-Lempers, and Simons, 1989). Third, when companies cut production or factories close, school services for children may be constrained by a narrowing tax base. As systems that are subject to social and economic change, contemporary families and schools have to grapple with the implications of a changing economy for their roles in socializing the next generation.

Overview of the Study

The recession of the early 1980s had a pervasive impact on communities in the industrial heartland of the United States where job terminations, cutbacks in the size of the work force, rollbacks of wages and benefits, employee concessions, and plant closings occurred in industries. This chapter summarizes the results of a study of parents and their early adolescents, Change in Parents' Work Lives and Adolescent Adjustment, conducted during the height of the recession in the Midwest. My first objective is to discuss some of the results of this work. A second goal is to raise the methodological questions encountered in the project as examples of problems inherent in conducting field studies of economic change.

The Transitions at Early Adolescence Project. The study of parents' changing work status was appended to a two-year, four-wave panel study, the Transitions at Early Adolescence Project (Eccles, 1988), an investigation of normative change (that is, the transition to junior high school) and its effects on early adolescents' attitudes and behavior. Parents, teachers, and principals participated in the study as well, providing independent sources of information about adolescent adjustment in two different developmental settings, the home and school.

The Transitions at Early Adolescence Study was conducted between 1983 and 1985 in twelve working-class and middle-class communities where auto and auto-related manufacturing were the main industries. Layoffs and plant closings had a pervasive impact in several of these communities as was evident in the official unemployment statistics, which ranged between 7.9 and 21 percent during the first wave of data collection. Since the focus of the study was on the relationship of changing environments to shifts in early adolescents' attitudes and behavior, a short-term longitudinal design was used. By expanding the context of the study beyond the immediate settings of early adolescent development and including information about changes in other areas of family life, specifically parents' paid employment, we were able to link events in the community to the settings of childhood (Bronfenbrenner, 1979).

The Transitions Project offered several advantages for a study of economic change and its effects on families and children. There were multiple sources of information (mothers, fathers, teachers, and adolescents) that provided a rich picture of adolescent adjustment. The longitudinal design meant that we could examine the dynamic nature of work and its relationship to family processes and adolescent adjustment over a two-year period. The design also offered a clear advantage over cross-sectional studies in supporting causal direction. Finally, the study was conducted during a major recessionary period when dislocations were common among families in the Midwest. There was broad variation in the sample families' exposure to economic change. Some were directly affected by loss while others enjoyed promotions or monetary gains. The largest group of families reported no changes in work status during the course of the study and served as a comparison group.

Three studies are discussed here. The first is a cross-sectional comparison relating parental work status at Wave I to socialization processes that shape adolescents' aspirations. In the second study longitudinal data are used to assess the effects of various transitions in work status (deprived, recovery, and stable) during the two years of the study on parent–adolescent authority relations. The third study uses data from elementary school principals and teachers to examine the impact of the recession on learning environments in the schools.

General information about the sample and procedures is followed by a discussion of specific hypotheses, analyses, and results for each study. In order to test different hypotheses, different subsets of the data were used; therefore, the number of cases varies due to the case selection criteria used in each analysis.

Sample. The target groups for the Transitions Study were sixth-graders, their teachers, and parents. Participating families were recruited through the schools. At Wave I, 79 percent of the eligible students participated; 95 percent of the sixth-grade teachers representing 143 classrooms participated, and at least one parent from 72 percent of the families that agreed to participate completed a questionnaire.

More than 93 percent of the families were Caucasian, approximately 4 percent were African American, and 3 percent were other minorities. Average family size was between two and three children. Forty-five percent of the fathers and 38 percent of the mothers had college or technical education beyond high school. Thirty-two percent of the mothers worked full time and another 24.5 percent worked part time. Seventy-five percent of the families were two-parent married families, 15 percent single-parent families, and 10 percent remarried families. Most fathers were employed in manual labor, sales, service, and professional jobs; working mothers were mainly employed in clerical, teaching, and service occupations (U.S. Department of Commerce, 1980).

Procedure. The Transitions Study was described as a study of changes in schools and families occurring during the early adolescent years. Project staff visited sixth-graders in their classrooms and the students were asked to carry permission letters to their parents. In the fall and spring of the 1983 and 1984 school years, questionnaires were administered to the adolescents as a group in their classrooms. Parents were mailed questionnaires with return postage envelopes for completion in their homes. Follow-up contacts included postcards and phone calls to parents.

Defining Parental Work Status. At Wave I, parents were given a list of potential changes in work status and were asked to check any that had occurred in their immediate family during the two-year period prior to Wave I. If they reported a layoff they were also asked how long the layoff period had been. Based on these responses, each family was coded in one of the following groups: promotion ($N = 382$); stable or no work-related changes ($N = 907$); temporarily (from one to eighteen months) laid off ($N = 231$); deskilled/demoted ($N = 149$); or permanently (longer than eighteen months) laid off ($N = 180$).

By assessing changes that had occurred in the two-year period prior to 1983—that is, the height of the recession—we captured a relatively large number of work-related changes. As the numbers show, the burden of economic change was not evenly distributed. Not only did some families report no changes, but others actually experienced an increase in status during the recession years. Indeed, the data suggest that one effect of recessions is a widening gap between social classes.

The coding scheme meant that the change in work status could have been the mother's, the father's, or both parents' since all of these changes were considered a disruption of the family's customary standards (Elder and Caspi, 1989). In fact, based on other variables in the data set, it appears that the majority of work-related changes were experienced by fathers. Eighteen months was used as a dividing line between temporary and permanent layoffs to assess different degrees of hardship. During the period of time we were studying, auto workers were eligible for unemployment compensation and supplementary unemployment benefits (SUB) that would last approximately one year.

In addition to the categories listed, parents were asked to report "any other changes in financial status." There were more than 600 answers to this open-ended item including "cutbacks of overtime," "pay concessions," "loss of a business," and "both parents now working." Most of these responses were elaborations on the changes noted in the closed-ended items. The fact that so many parents gave additional details suggests that they were quite willing to provide information about financial changes in a questionnaire that was essentially focused on early adolescent adjustment.

Disentangling Social Class and Parental Work Status. Not surprisingly, there was a highly significant relationship between parental work status and family income, $F(4, 1757) = 91.34$, $p < .0001$, and all but one of the between-group comparisons were highly significant ($p < .0001$). Promoted families had higher incomes than any other group. Stably employed families had higher incomes than those who experienced demotions or temporary or permanent layoffs. Income for the temporarily laid-off group was only slightly higher ($p < .05$) than for families in the demoted category, and those who reported a permanent layoff had the lowest income of any group.

The average level of mother's and father's education (mean parent education) was also strongly related to the work status categories, $F(4, 1844) = 26.79$, $p < .0001$). As in the income comparisons, mean parent education of the promoted group was significantly higher than for any other group. There were no differences in mean education of the stably employed and demoted families, but both of these groups had higher levels of education than parents in the temporary or permanent layoff categories. There were no differences in education between parents in the temporary and permanent layoff groups.

These results raised the question of confounds. That is, if parental work status is related to other indicators of a family's socioeconomic status (SES), are we studying the effects of changing work status or persistent factors of family background? The significant relationship between work status and income may mean that current family income reflects the change in parental work status that occurred during the previous two years. Alternatively, since both income and parents' education were related to work status, one could conclude that lower SES groups are more vulnerable to dislocations during periods of economic change.

In contrast to family income, parents' education is not subject to fluctuations in work attachment and can be interpreted as unidirectional in its effects (Bronfenbrenner, 1986). For this reason, parents' average education was used as a control for family background in the analyses. Although controlling for background effects clarifies statistical relationships, the substantive issue remains. That is, the independent variables may be confounded but they occur simultaneously in the lives of many children and have compound effects on their development.

Study 1: Parental Work Status and the Socialization of Adolescents' Aspirations

Parent's Roles as Achievement Models. There is a persistent relationship between parents' occupational and educational attainments and the parallel achievements of their children (Hauser and Featherman, 1977). The mechanisms by which this intergenerational transmission of socioeconomic attainment occurs are less clear. Undoubtedly, conditions in families such as size and income limit a child's identity exploration and restrict the possibilities he or she imagines for the future. Beyond these objective conditions, parents play a significant role in socializing the aspirations of their children. In their life-style and interactions they model occupational directions and may also define alternative paths for their children. Child-rearing styles evolve from economic and cultural reality. Parents in our sample were grappling with the implications of a changing economy in their lives, and we were interested in the relationship of these changes to child-rearing styles.

Since economic loss and unemployment are correlated with a lower sense of efficacy and control (Cohn, 1978), do they also undermine parents' confidence about preparing their sons and daughters for the future? When parents are coping with economic dislocations, are they less satisfied with their lives and do they urge their children to achieve more in life? Is the variation in adolescents' course enrollment plans and occupational aspirations related to changes in the work status of their parents? These were some of the questions that guided our study.

We asked mothers and fathers about several aspects of their role in socializing children's educational and occupational achievement. I present results for four of these variables: how satisfied they were with their own lives and accomplishments, whether they urged their son or daughter to achieve more in life, how confident they felt about helping their child prepare for the future, and whether they would encourage their son or daughter to get a college degree. In addition, we assessed early adolescents' aspirations by asking whether they planned to take nonrequired math courses and whether they planned to work full time, get vocational training, or complete a four-year college degree after high school graduation. Adolescents' "intentions to take more math courses" was included to assess the consistency of an adolescent's aspirations for the future with his or her present educational plans. That is, the educational direction of the junior high school student who expects to go to college but does not intend to take more math is not as clear as that of the student who realizes the importance of math courses for college admission. Parents' responses were measured on a 1-7 Likert scale and adolescents' responses on a 1-4 Likert scale.

Although we expected to find different patterns of socialization as a function of a status gain or loss, we did not hypothesize between-group differences for specific categories of status loss. However, socialization processes may vary according to the specific kind of loss a family experienced. Therefore, rather than aggregate the demoted, temporary, and permanent layoff categories into one "loss" group, we decided to explore these dimensions of work status loss on socialization processes.

In sum, mothers' and fathers' reports were analyzed separately as were adolescents' aspirations as a function of the five categories of work status. In the discussion I emphasize the overall pattern of results associated with family work status rather than focusing on group differences for each item. Indeed, for some variables there were significant between-group differences whereas for others the differences were marginal. If we want to understand the mechanisms underlying SES consistencies across generations, however, we have to get away from single outcome indicators (such as college aspirations) and examine more complex socialization patterns.

Results for Mothers and Fathers. As expected, patterns of achievement socialization differed as a function of a loss or gain in status. Mothers and fathers in promoted families were the most satisfied with their accomplishments and confident that they could prepare their children for the future. They were also the least likely of any group of parents to urge their children to achieve more in life but the most likely to expect their sons and daughters to go to college. Compared to the parents in promoted families, mothers and fathers in stable families had slightly lower means on these items but the differences were not statistically significant. The only exception was that mothers in stable families were significantly less confident about helping their children prepare for the future.

The more interesting differences, however, emerged in comparisons between categories of status loss. Compared with their peers who were demoted or permanently laid off, parents in the temporarily laid-off families were more satisfied with their lives; yet, like other parents who lost status, they urged their children to surpass their own achievements. Parents in the temporarily laid-off families were the least likely of any group to encourage their children to go to college, despite the fact that they had the highest incomes of any families who had lost status. Mothers, and especially fathers, were the least confident of any group about preparing their children for the future. In short, parents in temporarily laid-off families wanted their children to accomplish more in the future but did not know how to prepare them for the future and did not consider college a future goal.

In contrast, mothers and fathers in the demoted and permanently laid-off families were as likely as those in stable families to encourage their children to go to college. Mothers in the demoted families were also as confident as those in the promoted families that they could prepare their sons and daughters for the future. However, parents in the demoted and permanently laid-off families, especially fathers in the latter group, were the least satisfied with their lives and accomplishments. In sum, a loss of status had different implications for parents' roles as achievement models depending on the specific nature of the loss.

Results for Adolescents. Generally, the adolescents' aspirations reflected the patterns reported by their parents. Adolescents in promoted families had clear and consistent goals. More than any other group, they planned to go to college and to take additional math courses. Although they were as likely as any of their peers to want a full-time job after high school, they were the least likely to expect to get vocational training. Consistent with the picture provided by their well-educated parents who were satisfied with their lives and confident about preparing their children for the future, these sixth-graders were clearly set on a high-status track.

In contrast, the pattern for adolescents in temporarily laid-off families, while internally consistent, suggests a foreclosure of identity and a more limited view of future options. Consistent with their parents' scores (that is, the lowest on encouraging college and confidence in preparing for the future), this group was the least likely to intend to take more math or attend college but the most likely to plan on vocational training after high school. These aspirations mirror their parents' educational attainments. On average, parents in this group had some vocational training beyond high school. According to their teachers, adolescents in the temporarily laid-off families were as well adjusted at school as their peers in the promoted or stable families and significantly better adjusted than those in the permanently laid-off families. Nonetheless, they had the lowest academic aspirations of any group.

Adolescents whose parents were demoted held higher aspirations for academic achievement compared to peers in the temporarily laid-off families despite the lower income of the demoted families. Parental education was higher for this group and may be a more critical variable informing adolescents' aspirations. Not only did they intend to go to college, for example, but unlike their peers in permanently laid-off families, they also intended to enroll in more math courses and were less likely than their peers in the temporarily laid-off families to aspire to vocational training or a full-time job after high school.

Finally, adolescents in permanently laid-off families maintained high future aspirations but low achievement behaviors. Their college endorsements were as high as those of peers in the stable families, but they did not intend to take more math and, according to their teachers, were the most poorly adjusted adolescent group.

These early adolescents were a full five years from high school graduation, yet there was already an association of their parents' work status in the construction of their future plans. Other analyses of these data showed that financial pressures had an even stronger deleterious effect on girls' aspirations compared with boys' (Flanagan, 1989a).

The results indicate the utility of disaggregating the loss category. For example, although parents in the temporarily laid-off families were satisfied with their accomplishments relative to parents who experienced other kinds of status loss, they still urged their children to achieve more in life than they themselves had achieved. They were less likely to endorse college as a possible route to such achievements, however, despite the fact that they had higher incomes than the other "loss" families.

Likewise, it was useful to study adolescents' aspirations based on three different kinds of loss in parental work status. The adolescents in permanently laid-off families with the least resources maintained high aspirations for college, aspirations that appeared to be at odds with their behavior. (That is, they did not intend to take more math courses and, according to their teachers, were having problems adjusting to school.) In contrast, there was a consistency in the plans of adolescents whose parents experienced a temporary layoff. They expected to go to work or get vocational training but neither planned to take additional math courses nor planned to go to college after high school.

Long-Term Consequences of Hardship. Anecdotal evidence suggests that children from unemployed families learn to be less demanding and to constrict their aspirations to coincide with narrowing opportunities (United Community Services Public Hearings, 1983). Such adaptations to hardship may have enduring developmental implications. For example, a period of extended identity exploration may appear to be both a luxury and a risk that some children feel they cannot afford. Instead, children in hard-pressed homes may commit early in development to specific educational and occupational paths that ensure stability for their future. The low aspirations of adolescents in the temporarily laid-off families could be interpreted in this way. In fact, Elder (1974) reported that adolescents became more vocationally committed during the Depression when their family income suddenly dropped. As Moen, Kain, and Elder (1983) observe, "Economic adversity and adaptations to that misfortune become a legacy for members of the next generation, structuring in turn their options and resources for dealing with adversity, as well as the very shape of their lives" (p. 213).

Study 2: Economic Change and Parent-Adolescent Decision Making

Longitudinal Data. The results discussed thus far were obtained with data gathered at the first wave, and the implications are suggestive rather than conclusive. As a short-term panel design, the Transitions Study offered an advantage over cross-sectional studies by allowing us to test whether economic hardship was simply correlated with or actually had an effect on family relations and adolescent adjustment. During the two years of the study parents experienced positive and negative transitions in their work status. By forming categories based on the patterns of parents' changing work status during the two years of the study, we could relate transitions in the family's work status to patterns of change in the parent-adolescent relationship during the same time interval.

We identified the following four categories of family work status by comparing mothers' responses about changes that had occurred in the family at Wave I and Wave IV: a job loss or demotion with no recovery (the *deprived* group, N = 96), a loss or demotion followed by reemployment (the *recovery* group, N = 134), stable employment followed by a job loss or demotion during the study (the *declining* group, N = 107), and continuous employment (the *stable* group, N = 555).

Promotions were not included at Wave IV because we were more interested in studying recovery as a positive change in status. The total N listed next to each category was based on the total responses from mothers at Waves I and IV. The number of cases in the study discussed below is smaller (N = 504) due to missing data from mothers or adolescents at one of the four waves and due to the exclusion of families that had been promoted at Wave I.

In the next study, we compared three of these groups (deprived, recovery, and stable families). The number of declining-status families with complete data at all four waves was too small to include in the design. Repeated-measures analyses of covariance were used to assess the effects of these shifts in parental work status on patterns of parent-adolescent authority relationships during the two years of the study.

Parent-Adolescent Decision-Making Processes. A basic tenet of the study was that the strains of family hardship on children would be observable in the context of normative developmental tasks that are significant at different stages. One such transition occurs in parent-adolescent authority relations during early adolescence. Generally, parent-adolescent relations assume a certain reciprocity, a healthy give and take, as the adolescent's participation and independence in decision making gradually increases and parents relinquish some authority. Although this transition occurs with relatively little conflict, parents have to be willing to accommodate, to accept their adolescent's questioning and criticism of their rules and to bear with their children when they make mistakes. We expected that financial hardship occurring at this transition time would strain parents' capacity to be understanding, patient, and responsive to their adolescent's demands for an increased voice in decision making. We expected to find more tension between parents and adolescents over authority and independence issues and lower satisfaction among adolescents with their participation in decision making when parents were preoccupied with issues of family welfare.

Compensatory Effects of Reemployment. Several longitudinal studies have found that reemployment compensates for the increases in psychological distress and the tensions in marital relationships that individuals experience when they are laid off (Kessler, Turner, and House, 1989; Liem and Liem, 1989). We expected to find a similar compensatory effect on decision-making processes in the recovery group. That is, we predicted that reports of conflict would decline and that autonomy and satisfaction with decision making would increase when an adolescent's parent returned to work after a period of layoff.

Sex Differences. The transition in authority relationships at early adolescence tends to be marked by an increase in conflict noted by boys and an increase in emotional autonomy and self-reliance among girls (Douvan and Adelson, 1966; Steinberg and Silverberg, 1986). Based on the accentuation principle (Elder and Caspi, 1989), which states that financial hardship accentuates the distinguishing characteristics of individuals and relationships, we expected that financial hardship would exacerbate the gender differences noted above. That is, deprivation would intensify boys' conflict with their parents and dissatisfaction with their participation in decision making but would increase girls' autonomy and independence.

Decision-Making Measures. At each of the four waves, adolescents and their mothers were asked their perceptions of family decision-making practices. These items, based on an adaptation of Epstein and McPartland's (1977) Family Decision-Making Scale, formed two factors each for mothers and for adolescents: parent-adolescent conflict and adolescent autonomy. In addition, at Waves II, III, and IV adolescents were asked two questions about their ideal and real voice in family decision making: how much they felt they should be allowed to participate in making decisions, and how much they did in fact participate. Based on Lee's method (Lee, Statuto, and Kedar-Voivodas, 1983) for classroom decision making, a discrepancy or difference score was computed by subtracting the adolescent's actual level from his or her ideal level of participation in decision making. The adolescent's satisfaction with his or her decision-making participation was based on this discrepancy score. A large discrepancy or difference score indicates less satisfaction with the level of participation in decision making.

Results. As expected, financial hardship strained parent-adolescent authority relations. The deprived group had the highest reports of conflict over the two years of the study, and the recovery group showed the predicted compensatory effect of recovery over time. In fact, the only group to show significant declines in conflict and increases in satisfaction with their participation in decision making during the study were adolescents whose parents returned to work during the study. Adolescents' perceptions of autonomy were not as sensitive to the effects of changing work status over time. However, mothers in deprived families reported that their daughters experienced the highest levels of autonomy and independence of any adolescent group (Flanagan, in press).

There was a clear association of change in parental work status and adolescents' satisfaction with their participation in family decision making. Among the recovering families, adolescents reported increased satisfaction with their participation in decision making between Waves II and IV, $F(2, 198) = 4.42$, $p = .01$. The trend for adolescents in the deprived families was in the opposite direction—less satisfaction with their participation over waves, $F(2, 122) = 3.81$, $p = .03$. There were no differences between the deprived and recovery groups at Wave II (when both groups were dealing with economic declines), but significant differences between these groups emerged at Wave III, $F(1, 483) = 3.92$, $p = .05$, and increased at Wave IV, $F(1, 483) = 8.70$, $p = .003$, due to an increase in satisfaction for the recovery group and a decrease in satisfaction with decision making for the deprived group. In contrast to these patterns, there was no change in satisfaction among adolescents whose parents' work status remained stable. In sum, economic recovery was associated with lower conflict and more satisfaction among adolescents with their participation in decision making whereas deprivation increased strains in parent-adolescent authority relations.

As expected, family hardship accentuated normative gender differences in adolescents' autonomy and independence strivings documented in other research (Douvan and Adelson, 1966; Steinberg and Silverberg, 1986). Financial deprivation had a stronger impact on boys' reports of conflict with their parents than on girls' reports. Conversely, mothers tended to grant their daughters more autonomy than their sons and financial hardship accentuated this sex difference. In fact, daughters in deprived households participated significantly more in family decision making compared with any other adolescent group (Flanagan, in press). There were no sex differences in adolescents' satisfaction with their participation in decision making.

Since sons but not mothers in deprived households reported high levels of conflict, we suspect that boys' reports reflect increased conflict with their unemployed or demoted fathers. As Elder, Van Nguyen, and

Caspi (1985) found, financial hardship during the Great Depression increased boys' negative perceptions of and anger toward their unemployed fathers. In contrast to the patterns for sons, hardship increased the daughter's independence and the mother's respect for her daughter's opinions. Just as conditions in single-parent families cause children to "grow up a little faster" compared with peers in two-parent homes (Weiss, 1979), these data suggest that daughters in deprived families are pressed to participate in family decisions and to be independent at a younger age. In sum, the results of the longitudinal analyses suggest that short-term changes in work status affect the quality of parent-adolescent relationships. In addition, perceptions may vary due to the adolescent's gender and the position of the informant (mother or adolescent) in the authority relationship.

Study 3: Effects of the Recession on Schools

The debate on educational excellence has focused national attention on academic standards, teacher competency, and the poor performance of American students in international comparisons. However, it has all but ignored the impact that economic changes in communities exert on the opportunities that schools can provide for children. Since school systems depend largely on local property taxes, the economic fortunes of a community play a major role in the quality of its schools. When industries shut down or reduce their work force, a smaller property tax base means that schools are less able to provide children with a quality education. In addition, distressed communities are likely to find it increasingly difficult to get millage requests approved and schools are faced with belt-tightening measures. In short, whether or not a child's parents are directly affected by a layoff, an individual child's educational opportunities will be affected to the extent that his or her community has been hit by economic change.

We expected that the differential impact of the recession on communities in our sample would be associated with cutbacks and elimination of programs and personnel in school districts. At Wave I, surveys were sent to fifty-one elementary school principals from the twelve school districts in the study. Forty-nine completed surveys were returned. The survey was an extensive list of enrichment classes (such as art, music, library, computers) and support personnel (such as counselor, gym teacher, teacher aides) that are typical targets when school budgets must be trimmed. Principals were asked to check whether these programs had been cut back or eliminated in their district during the previous two years. In addition, principals were asked to comment on the teaching conditions (class size, teachers' break time) and general morale in their building. Finally, both the principals and participating sixth-grade teachers were asked two open-ended questions: What effect, if any, had changes in the state's economy had on their school, and what were their recommendations for improving education in the face of economic change?

Based on the unemployment statistics for their township, schools were categorized in the low (7 to 10 percent; $N = 6$), medium (11 to 14 percent; $N = 25$), or high (15 to 21 percent; $N = 18$) unemployment category. Given the small sample of schools and districts and the uneven number of schools falling in each of the unemployment categories, the results should be considered suggestive rather than conclusive.

Chi square tests of independence revealed a significant reduction of enrichment programs and support personnel in the medium- and high-unemployment categories compared with the program and personnel changes in schools in the low-unemployment category. No significant differences in teaching conditions such as increased class size were noted as a function of unemployment rates.

Due to the small pool of responses, we did not code the open-ended questions into categories but decided, instead, to use these comments as qualitative support for the link of economic change in communities to conditions in the schools. Both teachers and principals whose districts bore the brunt of the recession said that the state's changing economy had affected resources and the general level of stress in their schools. Teachers who taught in the middle- or high-unemployment areas, for example, reported a spillover effect of parental unemployment. They contended that children were more stressed and that their teaching duties had expanded because they were "filling in" for parents and providing emotional support to children. Teachers in hard-pressed school districts also perceived an increase in their work load since special classes such as gym and music had been eliminated. Not only had they lost preparation time due to the elimination of these classes, but some sixth-grade teachers were doing their best to provide these experiences to their students. Principals in these hard-pressed districts noted that the failure of recent millages meant a lack of funds for building repair and textbook and equipment purchases. One principal said that many of the parents were auto workers who had been unemployed for two years, had less money, and whose children had less interest in school. In contrast, in those districts where unemployment rates were relatively low, teachers and principals said there had been no effects of the recession in their schools.

Schools have historically been considered a great equalizer of opportunity in society. These descriptive data suggest that opportunities vary according to community resources and that such resources are subject to periods of economic change.

Conclusions

This study of change in parents' work lives was an attempt to locate early adolescents' development in a broad social context and to consider the implications of widespread economic change on the settings of childhood (Bronfenbrenner, 1979). The results suggest that although children are not participants in the world of work, they are not immune from the impact of economic change. If parents are laid off, demoted, or terminated from their jobs, family tensions may increase and parents are likely to be less responsive to children's developmental needs. Recessions can also exacerbate social class differences in the socialization of aspirations and in opportunities available in the home and at school, which may have long-term consequences for children's futures.

Methodological Issues. Recessionary periods can be useful times for studying how families and schools adapt to changing economic conditions, but there are challenges inherent in conducting such research. I turn now to a discussion of several methodological issues.

Definitions of Economic Change. Economic change can be operationally defined in several ways, and that definition is critical in understanding its meaning for families and children. Objective measures of economic change have been based primarily on a percentage of income loss (Elder, 1974; Chapter Two of this volume) or on declines in employment status (Flanagan, in press; Kessler, Turner, and House, 1989; Liem and Liem, 1989). In either case, the emphasis has been on *change* in a family's status in an attempt to distinguish such conditions from the persistent deprivations and strains of poverty.

A recent or sudden loss is stressful because families are faced with a disparity between their assumptions and their current conditions (Moen, Kain, and Elder, 1983). Coping with this disparity implies a subjective assessment of the family's objective conditions and an alternative definition of economic change. For example, Lempers, Clark-Lempers, and Simons (1989) used adolescents' perceptions of their family's economic hardship, a subjective assessment, as the independent variable in their study of adolescent adjustment. They contend that objective information about the extent of real income loss can be difficult to obtain, especially from children or adolescents, whereas life-style accommodations are salient indicators that the family is experiencing financial strain. Since perceptions of reality rather than objective conditions guide behavior, subjective assessments of deprivation tend to be more closely related than objective measures to other psychological indexes. In fact, subjective financial strains appear to mediate the relationship between job loss and adults' as well as children's ill health (Kelly, Sheldon, and Fox, 1985; Kessler, Turner, and House, 1989). All of the definitions discussed thus far, whether based on change in income, employment status, or subjective perceptions of hardship, rely on retrospective comparisons—that is, the family's current status compared with its former status. In contrast, longitudinal data provide a prospective approach to the study of economic change. With longitudinal designs we can uncover the dynamic nature of work including declines and recoveries in status and income. In addition, with measures of the key dependent variables at several time points, we can control for initial levels of the variables of interest and be more precise about the effects of economic change on behavior.

Regardless of the operational definition of economic change that one ultimately employs, the choice requires careful thought. All too often our knowledge has been based on comparisons of working versus nonworking people. As Chapter Five of this volume shows, a static definition of unemployment fails to capture such variables as underemployment or job discouragement. Finally, in an effort to distinguish economic declines from poverty, we must be careful not to draw artificial lines between groups if the least skilled workers and the working poor are, in fact, the most vulnerable to economic downturns.

Selection Bias. The second methodological issue, selection bias, poses a problem for two reasons. First, as Kessler, Turner, and House (1989) note, individual problems such as ill health can be predisposing factors that bias selection into unemployment. A second type of bias is due to self-selection into studies rather than selection into unemployment. Families that lack financial resources or social support are the most at risk during hard times and, undoubtedly, are less inclined to participate in studies. Despite the fact that they are overrepresented in unemployment statistics (McLoyd, in press), minorities are still underrepresented in studies of economic change and children.

Sample Attrition in Longitudinal Studies. Sample attrition creates bias in longitudinal studies. When families are faced with dislocation, the actual loss of income or job demotion is only one of many changes they will face in a period of a few years. For example, unemployment is known to be a contributing factor in marital dissolutions (Ross and Sawhill, 1975). In short, families who remain in a longitudinal study are likely to have more resources and fewer strains compared with those who drop out.

Studying attrition cases with longitudinal data is one way to assess sample bias. Using the longitudinal data in the Transitions Study we were able to compare families that remained in the study for four waves with those that were present at Wave I but dropped out at subsequent waves. This comparison showed that the attrition group had fewer resources measured in terms of income, parent education, and family structure (single-parent or two-parent), as well as more demands on their time due to larger family size and more working mothers. Although we obtained statistically meaningful results with the longitudinal data, we suspect that the findings underrepresent the effects of economic hardship in the general population.

Control Groups. The absence of comparison groups of continuously employed families or families with stable income has been a serious oversight in some studies of economic change, one that compromises the interpretation of results. Without control groups, there is no objective basis for assessing the impact of economic change on family relationships or on individual behavior. In developmental studies, control groups representing a normal range of developmentally appropriate behavior provide the only valid basis for assessing adjustment problems.

Multiple Sources of Information. In the second study discussed in this chapter, we found that adolescents' reports of conflict were related to changes in their family's work status but mothers' reports did not reflect a similar relationship. Mothers, however, reported that deprivation increased pressures on daughters to be independent although daughters did not note this association. These conflicting perceptions underscore the importance of obtaining multiple perspectives from family members or from significant individuals such as teachers who can assess children's adjustment outside of the family setting. Relying on only one source for reports of economic change and perceptions of family processes and personal adjustment poses the problem of confounding between the independent and dependent variables. For example, parents who feel the strains of hardship may perceive more adjustment problems in their children, whereas neither teachers nor children notice such difficulties. In this case, the dependent variable is probably tapping parental anxiety and, as such, it is an invalid measure of children's adjustment.

Designing Prospective Studies. Two goals of social science research are a broader understanding of family systems and human adaptation to change. With these goals in mind, researchers need to focus attention on the events outside the family that affect interpersonal processes within the family setting. There are several ways that we can gather data to build this knowledge base.

The designs of prospective developmental studies, particularly longitudinal ones, could enlarge their scope to include relevant family measures. At least some basic demographics as well as life event and family process measures should be included so that economic transitions in families can be studied in the context of normative developmental change. Likewise, since characteristics of individuals and their relationships moderate the impact of stressors on adjustment, they too should be included in the study design. For example, personality characteristics may buffer early adolescents despite their family's exposure to hardship (Flanagan, 1989b).

An awareness of potential change within the communities where field studies are conducted can broaden the base of important variables to include in a prospective design. Unlike natural disasters, there are often precipitating events to the economic downturns in a community. Many plant closings, for example, can be predicted well in advance of the actual termination; in fact, workers must now be officially informed sixty days prior to termination. One lesson learned from research on the Great Depression is that the impact of labile events on human development can be uncovered in the course of conducting normal longitudinal studies. The fact that both the Oakland Growth and Berkeley Guidance studies were longitudinal studies in progress when the Depression occurred meant that there were assessments of parents and children prior to the Depression. The specific effects of sudden hardship on family relationships and children's development could be disentangled from other personality and family system variables.

This research objective requires an interdisciplinary approach to research design, asking questions that enrich the data base of prospective studies and gathering opinions from many sources. A critical evaluation of what we know can assist in defining new directions for research. We have some information about the disorganizing effects of unemployment on family life; we know less about how families eventually accommodate and whether the daily lives of children are different as a result.

What adaptive responses do families make to economic change, and what consequences do these coping measures have for children in the long run? The longitudinal evidence discussed in this chapter suggests that some families recover after a temporary setback. We need more information about the structural conditions as well as the personal attributes that facilitate financial recovery. Furthermore, we need to examine how social and economic changes alter parents' beliefs about themselves and the world and whether such changes in parental belief systems affect their socialization practices. Faced with a profound loss of control over their work lives, do some parents resign themselves to fate? Do others use such setbacks in their adult lives to their child's motivational advantage, encouraging educational and occupational achievements? Does insecurity in their parents' work life cause children to live more contingent, less self-determined lives? The trends outlined in this chapter suggest the need for dynamic models of children's socialization and development, models that depart from a static "social address" paradigm and attend to historical changes as they affect the settings of childhood (Bronfenbrenner, 1986).

References

Bronfenbrenner, U. *The Ecology of Human Development: Experiments by Nature and Design.* Cambridge, Mass.: Harvard University Press, 1979.
Bronfenbrenner, U. "Ecology of the Family as a Context for Human Development: Research Perspectives." *Developmental Psychology,* 1986, *22* (6), 723–742.

Cohn, R. "The Effect of Employment Status Change on Self-Attitudes." *Social Psychology*, 1978, *41*, 81-93.
Dew, M. A., Bromet, E. J., and Schulberg, H. C. "A Comparative Analysis of Two Community Stressors' Long-Term Health Effects." *American Journal of Community Psychology*, 1987, *15*, 167-184.
Douvan, E., and Adelson, J. *The Adolescent Experience.* New York: Wiley, 1966.
Eccles, J. S. *Psychological and Behavioral Underpinnings of Performance.* Washington, D.C.: National Institute of Child Health and Human Development Final Report, 1988.
Elder, G. H., Jr. *Children of the Great Depression.* Chicago: University of Chicago Press, 1974.
Elder, G. H., Jr., and Caspi, A. "Economic Stress in Lives: Developmental Perspectives." *Journal of Social Issues*, 1989, *44*, 25-45.
Elder, G. H., Jr., Van Nguyen, T., and Caspi, A. "Linking Family Hardship to Children's Lives." *Child Development*, 1985, *56*, 361-375.
Epstein, J. L., and McPartland, J. M. *Family and School Interactions and Main Effects on Affective Outcomes.* (Report no. 235.) Baltimore, Md.: Center for Social Organization of Schools, Johns Hopkins University, 1977.
Flanagan, C. A. "Economic Stress in the Family: Do the Effects for Daughters and Sons Differ?" Paper presented at the biennial meeting of the Society for Research on Child Development, Kansas City, April 1989a.
Flanagan, C. A. "Parental Work Status and Early Adolescents' School Adjustment." Manuscript submitted for publication, 1989b.
Flanagan, C. A. "Change in Family Work Status: Effects on Parent-Adolescent Decision Making." *Child Development*, in press.
Harold, R., Radin, N., and Eccles, J. S. "Objective and Subjective Reality: The Effects of Job Loss and Financial Stress on Fathering Behaviors." *Family Perspective*, 1988, *22*, 309-326.
Harrison, B., and Bluestone, B. *The Great U-Turn: Corporate Restructuring and the Polarizing of America.* New York: Basic Books, 1988.
Hauser, R. M., and Featherman, D. L. *The Process of Stratification: Trends and Analysis.* New York: Academic Press, 1977.
Kelly, R., Sheldon, A., and Fox, G. L. "The Impact of Economic Dislocation on the Health of Children." In J. Boulet, A. M. DeBritto, and S. A. Ray (eds.), *The Impact of Poverty and Unemployment on Children.* Ann Arbor: University of Michigan Bush Program in Child Development and Social Policy, 1985.
Kessler, R. C., Turner, J. B., and House, J. S. "Effects of Unemployment on Health in a Community Survey: Main, Modifying, and Mediating Effects." *Journal of Social Issues*, 1989, *44*, 69-85.
Lee, P. C., Statuto, C. M., and Kedar-Voivodas, G . "Elementary School Children's Perceptions of Their Actual and Ideal School Experience: A Developmental Study." *Journal of Educational Psychology*, 1983, *75* (6), 839-847.
Lempers, J. D., Clark-Lempers, D., and Simons, R. L. "Economic Hardship, Parenting, and Distress in Adolescence." *Child Development*, 1989, *60*, 25-39.
Liem, R., and Liem, J. H. "The Psychological Effects of Unemployment on Workers and Their Families." *Journal of Social Issues*, 1989, *44*, 87-105.
McLoyd, V. C. "The Impact of Economic Hardship on Black Families and Children: Psychological Distress, Parenting, and Socioemotional Development." *Child Development*, in press.
Moen, P. "Unemployment, Public Policy, and Families: Forecasts for the 1980s." *Journal of Marriage and the Family*, 1983, *45*, 751-766.
Moen, P., Kain, E. L., and Elder, G. H. "Economic Conditions and Family Life:

Contemporary and Historical Perspectives." In R. R. Nelson and F. Skidmore (eds.), *American Families and the Economy: The High Costs of Living.* Washington, D.C.: National Academy Press, 1983.

Ross, H. L., and Sawhill, L. Y. *Time of Transition: The Growth of Families Headed by Women.* Washington, D.C.: Urban Institute, 1975.

Steinberg, L. D., and Silverberg, S. B. "The Vicissitudes of Autonomy in Early Adolescence." *Child Development,* 1986, 57, 841-851.

United Community Services. Public hearings on the special needs of children of the unemployed, Detroit, Michigan, November 1983.

U.S. Department of Commerce, Bureau of the Census. *Classified Index of Industries and Occupations.* Washington, D.C.: Government Printing Office, 1980.

Weiss, R. "Growing Up a Little Faster: The Experience of Growing Up in a Single-Parent Household." *Journal of Social Issues,* 1979, 35, 97-111.

Constance A. Flanagan is an assistant professor of psychology at the University of Michigan-Dearborn, where she directs the Women's Studies Program.

Income loss leads to lower family integration, which in turn makes adolescents more sensitive to evaluation by peers. This can result in lower self-esteem and an inclination to act against common rules and norms.

Family Income Loss and Economic Hardship: Antecedents of Adolescents' Problem Behavior

Rainer K. Silbereisen, Sabine Walper, Helfried T. Albrecht

> Now that we in psychology have turned our attention to the totality of human life and to men's close dependence on the environment, people living under the most diverse conditions, including those of extreme destitution, must become the subject of psychological inquiry.
> —Hildegard Hetzer (1929)

In this chapter we report on a series of studies designed to investigate effects of income loss on family relations and adolescents' proneness to problem behavior. The research is part of the Berlin Youth Longitudinal Study, an investigation of personality development in adolescence and young adulthood. The aim of the study is to analyze the role of problem behavior in normal adolescent development. Risk and protective factors

---

We would like to dedicate this chapter to Hildegard Hetzer, professor emerita at the University of Giessen, one of the pioneers in the study of economic hardship and human development, who celebrated her ninetieth birthday on June 9, 1989. The research was supported in part by German Research Council grants to R. K. Silbereisen (Si 293/1-1 through 6, co-investigator K. Eyferth; Si 296/3-1). Special thanks are extended to Lisa Crockett for helpful comments on an earlier version of this chapter and to Friedrich Fuhrmann for his technical assistance. Address correspondence to the authors at University of Giessen, Department of Psychology, Otto Behaghel Strasse 10 F, D-6300 Giessen, Federal Republic of Germany.

within the individual, and within family, work, and leisure contexts, have been investigated in Berlin (West Germany) and Warsaw (Poland). By 1989, one of the cohorts (a total of three per city) had been followed up once every year from age eleven to eighteen. (For a short technical reference see Verdonik and Sherrod, 1984.)

Background of the Research

Income loss due to unemployment is one of the negative side effects of the economic and technical changes that have occurred during the past ten to fifteen years. By 1983, the number of unemployed in West Germany was more than 2.2 million (the unemployment rate was 9 percent), and it has remained at this high level until very recently (Heinelt, Wacker, and Welzer, 1987). About two-thirds of the German unemployed aged twenty-five and above were living with their (married) partner, half of the latter with children under the age of fifteen (Breuer, Schoor-Theisen, and Silbereisen, 1984).

Unemployment figures tell only half of the story, since occupational downward mobility, reduced working hours, and loss of business for the self-employed contribute to the larger problem of family income loss. Research from the Great Depression in Germany and the United States has stressed the psychological significance of economic deprivation, be it due to unemployment or other causes (Jahoda, Lazarsfeld, and Zeisel, 1975; Angell, 1936; Cavan and Ranck, 1969; Elder, 1974).

Social changes occurring in Germany since the 1930s have produced some differences in the background against which economic hardship in the 1980s must be seen. First, government agencies today provide better financial support and improved health services. Nevertheless, after twelve months of unemployment only 56 percent of the previous income is paid to those who qualify for support. Second, the rise in maternal employment indicates changes in the family system and related norms and values that may affect a family's capacity to cope with economic deprivation. We must note, however, that the maternal employment rate in West Germany is not comparable with that in the United States. Whereas in 1985 more than 50 percent of American mothers with small children were in the labor force (Scarr, 1989), the corresponding figure was only 35 percent in West Germany (Statistisches Bundesamt, 1988).

According to Elder (1974), it is the relative decrease in a family's financial assets that leads to a "problematic disparity between the claims of a family in a situation and its control of outcomes, or, more specifically, . . . a gap between the socioeconomic needs and the ability to satisfy them" (p. 9). Since parents are responsible for the economic security of the family, they are seen as being directly affected by economic deprivation. Children's personality development, on the other hand, is supposed to be influenced indirectly by financial hardship; strained family relationships and impaired parent–child interaction are thought to provide the mediating link. Because attempts to cope with financial problems depend on the availability of material, social, and personal resources, the impact of economic deprivation is moderated by such factors as social class, previous family relations, and children's competencies. The role of family relationships and coping resources is most clearly documented in Elder's studies on the Great Depression (Elder, Caspi, and Downey, 1984; Elder, Liker, and Cross, 1984; Elder, Van Nguyen, and Caspi, 1985; Elder, Caspi, and Van Nguyen, 1986).

Based on earlier research, two main questions will be asked in this chapter: What is the role of mediating factors such as strained family relationships in linking the effects of economic hardship to changes in individual characteristics? What is the role of moderating factors such as educational resources in explaining individual differences concerning the impact of economic hardship? The remainder of the chapter is organized into four parts. In comparing families who experienced income loss with matched controls, we first address the influence of economic deprivation on family relationships, particularly family integration. Change in family integration is then considered as mediating adolescents' reactions to family income loss. To shed light on potential buffers of strain, we then examine contextual as well as personal resources. Finally, we report additional evidence from a study using a larger sample not specifically selected according to income change.

Study 1: Effects of Income Loss on Family Relationships

Liker and Elder (1983) have shown that financial conflicts as well as fathers' increased irritability contributed to the deterioration of marital relations among deprived families. Mothers' well-being, however, seemed largely unaffected by income loss, most likely because mothers felt less responsible for their family's economic difficulties.

Economic "failure" by the breadwinner seems to force a redefinition of roles (Anderson, 1980; Larson, 1984). Not only the father's loss of status and prestige within the family, but also the mother's complementary gain in influence over family affairs, reflect adaptive changes that are difficult to cope with and, therefore, increase tension (Bakke, 1969; Elder, 1974).

Our focus is on family integration, specifically the overall quality of cohesion and emotional bonds in the family system (Moos, 1974). Based on results of earlier studies, we expected, first, that an increase in the mother's influence would mediate the negative impact of income loss on family integration and, second, that due to a more equal distribution of family responsibilities today, mothers and fathers would be similarly affected by income loss. For both parents, psychological strains would lead to impaired family integration.

Method. The study took place in West Berlin, a large city with a population of almost two million. Data came from both parents as well as from the adolescent child, who was interviewed separately. (In Study 1 only parental data were used.) The adolescents' questionnaire assessment was conducted at school. The parents received mailed questionnaires consisting of a household questionnaire (to be filled out collaboratively by both parents) and separate parts for mother and father.

Sample. The sample comprises 134 families who were selected from 677 intact families participating in the first wave (1982–1983) of assessments. Due to missing data, especially in parents' responses, the actual sample size varies according to the variables used. (As in all waves, the adolescents were assessed October through December. For technical reasons the parents' data were gathered about two months later. Note that most parental data refer to the past year.)

Selection was done by including all sixty-seven families who reported a loss in family income during the year prior to the assessment and sixty-seven families whose income was stable (see below). These families were individually matched on both parents' education and occupational position, mother's employment status, the number of rooms per person in the family's home, and the adolescent's age and gender. The age of the adolescents in the sample ranged from ten to sixteen years (median: 12.2 years); boys and girls were equally represented.

Measures. *Income loss* was assessed in the household questionnaire. Parents reported changes in total family income during the past year. Changes of ±5 percent (considered "no loss") were coded as 0; changes of more than 5 percent and up to 25 percent ("moderate loss") were coded as 1; and changes of more than 25 percent ("high loss") were coded as 2. The data on income change can be considered valid, as parents also reported a decrease in their household expenditures (Walper, 1988).

Parents' strains were measured by the same two items for mothers and fathers. They reflected an increase in psychological tension during the past year. (For example: "During the last year, I have increasingly felt that I cannot cope with my tasks.") The correlation between the two items was higher for fathers ($r = .59$) than for mothers ($r = .30$).

Mother's influence on decision making in the family was based on the father's reports on three items, each concerning a different aspect of decision making (financial matters, issues concerning the children, and other important family affairs). A dichotomous variable was created indicating whether, during the past year, the mother gained influence in at least one aspect (1) or not at all (0).

Family integration was measured by four items for mothers and three items for fathers that are not identical in wording but represent the same factor. (Example for mothers: "In our family, there is a lot of friction"; inverted example for fathers: "In our family, everything is harmonious and peaceful.") Considering the small number of items, the internal consistency of α = .58 and .59 for mothers and fathers, respectively, is acceptable (see Nunally, 1967).

Results. Only ninety-nine families with complete data sets were available for the following analyses. Of these, twenty-two reported an income loss of more than 25 percent during the previous year, nineteen lost between 5 and 25 percent, and fifty-eight families reported stable income. Father's—but not mother's—education, occupation, and employment status were most predictive of family income loss, indicating that the reduced income was due mainly to the father's loss of earnings.

To test the mediating influence of parents' strains and mothers' influence on decision making, path analyses were conducted using a series of multiple regression analyses. The effects of income loss were taken into account using dummy variables, effect-coded (Cohen and Cohen, 1975). One dummy variable represented the effect of stable income versus loss of any size; the other represented the effect of high income loss versus moderate loss or stable income. Entered simultaneously into the regression, each effect is estimated independently of the other.

Figure 1 shows the path models; coefficients for mothers are given above each path and those for fathers below the paths. The effects of income loss on family integration without simultaneously assessing the effect of the mediators are given in parentheses.

With respect to our first hypothesis, high income loss is indeed predictive of the mother's increasing influence on decision making, which, in turn, corresponds to lower family integration. Furthermore, in line with our second hypothesis, income loss affects not only the father's but also the mother's well-being, and such increasing strains contribute to lower family integration. The strong advantage of stable-income families suggests that it is not only high income loss that is associated with higher strains, but loss of any size. Finally, if both mediators are taken into account, the direct effect of income loss on family integration is no longer significant. Further analyses (see Walper, 1988) also looked at the mother's self-perceived increasing decision-making power. We found no relation with income change. However, fathers' and mothers' judgments seem to be based on different criteria. Whereas restrictions in household expenditures were most relevant for fathers' attributions, mothers reported increasing decision-making power if they spent more time on household duties than before.

Figure 1. Parents' Increased Strains and Mothers' Increased Influence as Mediating Link Between Economic Deprivation and Family Integration

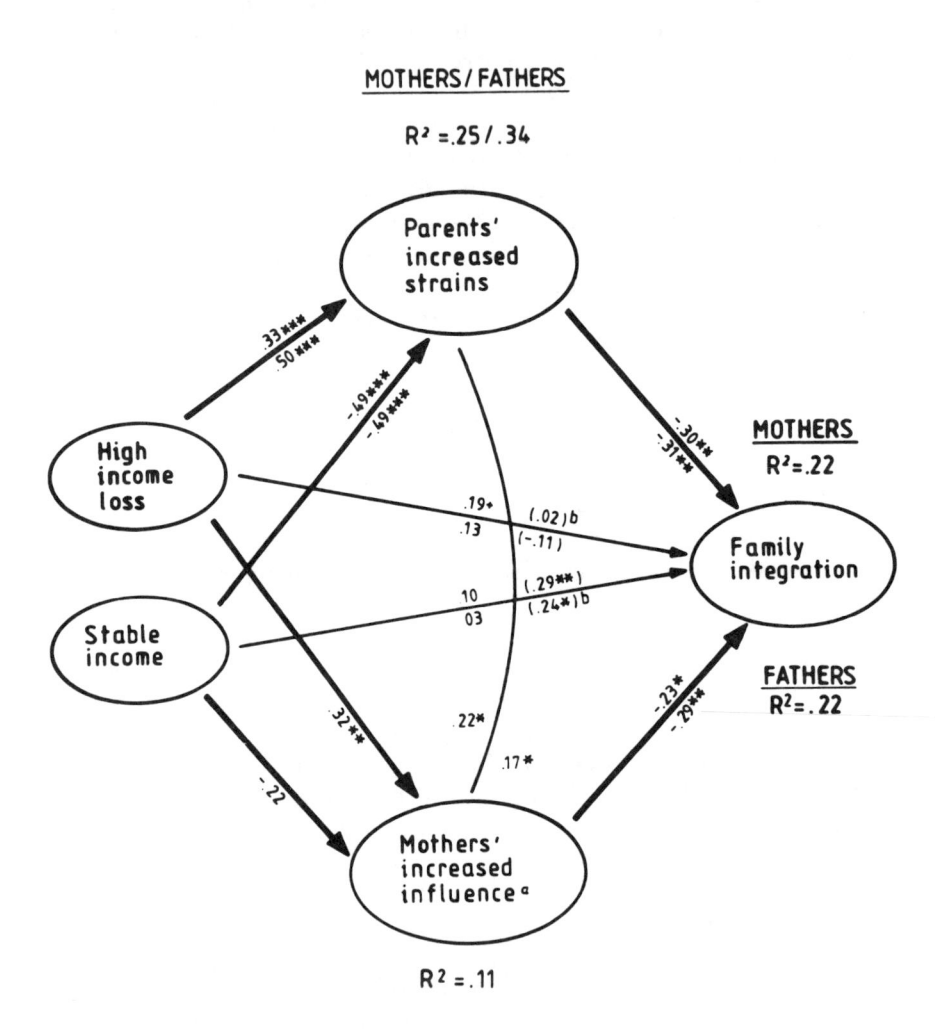

MOTHERS / FATHERS

$R^2 = .25 / .34$

[Path diagram with nodes: "High income loss", "Stable income", "Parents' increased strains", "Mothers' increased influence[a]", "Family integration"]

MOTHERS $R^2 = .22$

FATHERS $R^2 = .22$

$R^2 = .11$

Path coefficients shown:
- High income loss → Parents' increased strains: .33*** / .50***
- Stable income → Parents' increased strains: −.49*** / −.49***
- Parents' increased strains → Family integration: −.30** / −.37***
- High income loss → Family integration: .19+ / .13 (.02)[b] / (−.11)
- Stable income → Family integration: .10 / .03 (.29**) / (.24*)[b]
- Stable income → Mothers' increased influence: −.22
- High income loss → Mothers' increased influence: .32**
- Parents' increased strains → Mothers' increased influence: .22*
- Mothers' increased influence → Family integration: .17*
- Mothers' increased influence → Family integration: −.23* / −.29**

Note: Standardized regression coefficients for mothers are given above (and fathers below) the depicted paths. "Stable income" indicates the contrast between no change and loss of any kind; "high loss" indicates the contrast between high loss (more than 25 percent) and medium loss or unchanged income.

[a] Only fathers' judgment considered.

[b] Direct effects of economic deprivation on family integration omitting mediating effects.

+$p < .10$; *$p < .05$; **$p < .01$; ***$p < .001$.

Study 2: The Family as Mediator of Adolescent Transgression

Here we address the issue of whether the impact of economic hardship on adolescents' transgression proneness, that is, their willingness to break norms and rules of conduct, is mediated by family integration and adolescents' self-derogation (low self-esteem). Earlier studies led us to predict that impaired family integration mediates the impact of economic deprivation on adolescents' proneness to problem behavior (Elder, Liker, and Cross, 1984; Elder, Caspi, and Downey, 1984). In those studies, increasingly arbitrary discipline on the part of deprived fathers, and more punitive behavior by both parents, triggered by increased emotional instability and marital strain, provided the link between income loss and children's rebelliousness against parental authority and the adult world in general.

Self-derogation will be considered as an additional link. Earlier research has shown that daughters of unemployed fathers reported more emotional strain and more feelings of loneliness than daughters of employed fathers (Schindler and Wetzels, 1985). According to Elder, Van Nguyen, and Caspi (1985), deprived adolescent boys showed more anger reactions while girls tended to report worries and weeping over their sad feelings. Since such emotional strain should be reflected in low self-esteem (Blyth, Simmons, and Carlton-Ford, 1983), one could expect a direct effect of economic deprivation on self-derogation. Considering the influence of family cohesion on self-esteem (Cooper, Holman, and Braithwaite, 1983), however, an indirect influence of hardship on self-derogation (low self-esteem), mediated through family integration, seems more plausible.

Concerning transgression of societal norms and rules, it has been shown that self-derogation leads to deviant behavior, most likely by motivating the adolescent to search for an alternative to negative experiences in the normative reference group (Kaplan, 1980). Although it has been found in longitudinal studies (McCarty and Hoge, 1984) that breaking norms can have a debilitating effect on self-esteem, this seems not to be likely, when the effects of transgression proneness on self-esteem are considered instead of deviant behavior itself.

Finally turning to possible risk groups, research on coping with critical life events suggests that the effects of economic deprivation should be more pronounced among families with lower socioeconomic and problem-solving resources (Kessler, 1979; Liem and Liem, 1978). Hence four hypotheses are suggested. First, deprived adolescents will evidence higher transgression proneness than adolescents from stable-income families. Second, this increased transgression proneness will be mediated by higher self-derogation among deprived youth. Third, the impact of income loss on adolescents' self-derogation will be mediated by lower family integration. Fourth, families with less educated parents will suffer more.

Method. The same sample was used as in Study 1. Income loss was assessed in the same way, and family integration was measured by a combined index averaging mothers' and fathers' scores ($\alpha = .72$).

Educational level refers to a combination of both parents' education. Families in which parents had completed the lowest educational track in school (nine years of education) or in which one parent had not passed the final class of this track, regardless of the other parent's level of education, form the group low in education ($N = 51$). The other families constitute the group high in parental education ($N = 50$).

Self-derogation was measured by adolescents' response to four items adapted from Kaplan's (1980) scale (for example, "I think that I am not worth much"; $\alpha = .63$; see Silbereisen, Reitzler, and Zank, 1986).

Transgression proneness was assessed by three items concerning the adolescent's inclination to act against common rules and norms (for example, "I often find the rules and laws of adults bad and don't like to follow them"; $\alpha = .53$; see Galambos and Silbereisen, 1987). The predictive validity of the scale has been repeatedly demonstrated. Zank (1988), for instance, found more experimental use of inhalants among adolescents who reported higher transgression proneness in the previous year.

Results. Only 101 families with complete data sets were available for the following analyses. Using multiple regression techniques, separate path analyses were conducted for the two educational groups. The dummy variables of income change (see Study 1) and adolescent's gender (0 = male, 1 = female) serve as predictors, and family integration and self-derogation are used as mediators (see Walper and Silbereisen, 1987a). The full path models are given in Figure 2. Paths are depicted if $p < .10$ in one of the groups. The effects of income change on transgression proneness (before including the two mediating variables) are given in parentheses.

Concerning the less educated families, the results are in line with our expectations. As predicted in hypothesis 1, stable income (as opposed to loss of any size) is indeed related to lower transgression proneness among adolescents. (See the coefficients in parentheses.) Furthermore, in line with hypotheses 2 and 3, family integration and self-derogation seem to mediate this effect. Families with stable income report better family integration, which, in turn, contributes to reduced self-derogation, and self-derogation finally emerges as the only significant link to transgression proneness. In addition, there is a direct effect of high income loss on self-derogation, suggesting that an adolescent's well-being is not only influenced through family integration.

Concerning the more highly educated families, only the effects between family integration and self-derogation, and between self-deroga-

Figure 2. Effects of Economic Deprivation on Family Integration, Self-Derogation (Low Self-Esteem), and Transgression Proneness for Low and High Parental Education

HIGH PARENTAL EDUCATION (N=50)

[Path diagram: Stable income → Family integration (.23); High loss → Family integration (.15); Gender (f) → Family integration (+.32*); Stable income → Self-derogation; High loss → Self-derogation (+.09); Gender (f) → Self-derogation; Family integration → Self-derogation (-.28†); Self-derogation → Transgression proneness (+.41**); High loss → Transgression proneness (.01(.07)). $R^2=.07$ for Family integration; $R^2=.17$ for Self-derogation; $R^2=.12$ for Transgression proneness.]

LOW PARENTAL EDUCATION (N=51)

[Path diagram: Stable income → Family integration (.32*); High loss → Family integration (.34*); Gender (f) → Family integration; Stable income → Self-derogation; High loss → Self-derogation (+.34*); Gender (f) → Self-derogation (-.11); Family integration → Self-derogation (-.28†); Self-derogation → Transgression proneness (+.55***); High loss → Transgression proneness (-.21(-.36*)). $R^2=.22$ for Family integration; $R^2=.21$ for Self-derogation; $R^2=.44$ for Transgression proneness.]

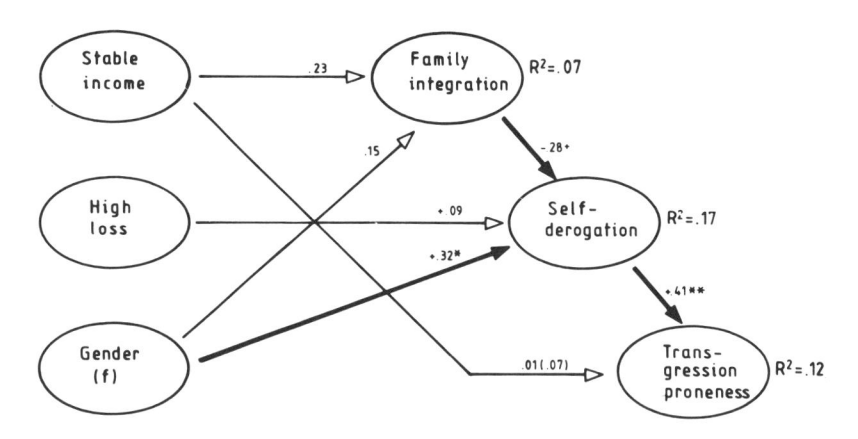

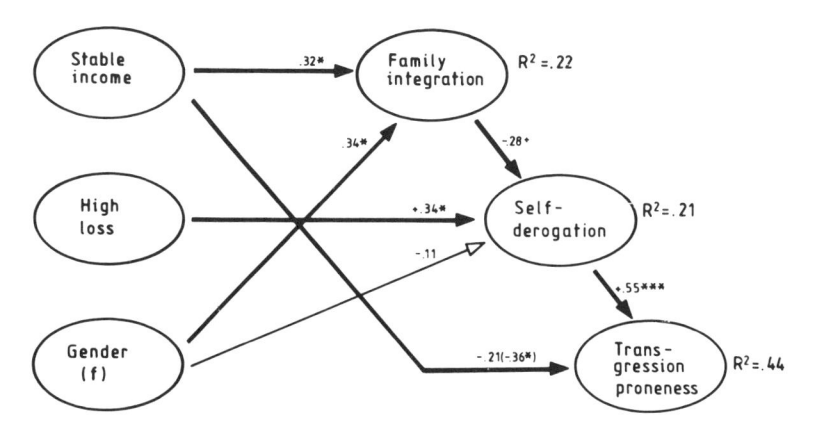

Note: Standardized regression coefficients are shown. Paths significant in at least one group are depicted.

†$p < .10$; *$p < .05$; **$p < .01$; ***$p < .001$.

tion and transgression proneness, are significant. Does this mean that we have indeed a different pattern of effects depending on educational resources? In order to investigate this question, we used LISREL (Jöreskog and Sörbom, 1984) and estimated the same structural model for both groups. This resulted in a good fit ($\chi^2 = 17.65$, $df = 21$, n.s.); thus the differences in effects between the two groups (concerning size and sign of path coefficients) are not systematic. Though additional analyses, using post hoc modifications of the model, point to group differences concerning the effect of high loss and gender on self-derogation, the chain of effects between loss, family integration, self-derogation, and transgression proneness does not differ for the two educational groups. Thus hypothesis 4 could not be confirmed.

Study 3: Personal Risk in Coping with Economic Hardship

Here we focus on adolescents' sensitivity to evaluations by significant others, particularly classmates, friends, and parents (see Fenigstein, Scheier, and Buss, 1975). Adolescents high in sensitivity to evaluation by others are seen as especially vulnerable to negative effects of income loss on self-derogation. Income loss puts restrictions on expenditures for all family members. Concerns about an unfavorable appearance due to less expensive and less fashionable clothing were reported for deprived adolescents (Elder, 1974; Schindler and Wetzels, 1985). Assuming that deprived youth who are highly attentive to others' evaluations are more affected by stigmatization and disapproval from peers, their self-esteem could be directly affected by economic hardship, independent of the influence of family relations. Furthermore, adolescents high in sensitivity to evaluation by others may suffer more from the increased tension and conflict in the family resulting from economic hardship.

Accordingly, our hypotheses are as follows. First, income loss is negatively related to family integration. Second, impaired family integration should provide the mediating link to adolescents' self-derogation only among those high in sensitivity to significant others, while their less sensitive agemates should remain unaffected. Third, highly self-sensitive adolescents should evidence an additional direct impact of economic deprivation on self-derogation that is not mediated by family integration. Fourth, self-derogation should mediate the effects of income loss and family integration on adolescents' transgression proneness irrespective of their sensitivity to significant others.

Method. The same sample was used as in Study 1. Income loss, family integration, self-derogation, transgression proneness, and gender were measured and scored as before.

Sensitivity to evaluation by significant others was measured by four items. (For example, "I become curious when others talk about me"; "When my classmates talk about me, I pay attention and want to know what they are saying"; see Silbereisen, Reitzler, and Zank, 1986, for further information.) The internal consistency of this scale was $\alpha = .71$.

To test the hypothesized moderating effect, the sample was split at the median, resulting in a group of adolescents high ($N = 47$) and a group of adolescents low ($N = 51$) in sensitivity to evaluation by significant others. (These groups do not differ on family income loss, parental education, adolescent's gender, mean age, family integration, and self-derogation. The only mean difference pertains to transgression proneness, with highly self-conscious adolescents reporting a greater inclination to act against common norms and rules.)

Results. Only ninety-eight families with complete data sets were available for the following analyses. Rather than computing ordinary path analyses, this time we applied the LISREL multiple group comparison approach (Jöreskog and Sörbom, 1984) to detect differences between the groups low and high in sensitivity to evaluation by significant others (see Walper and Silbereisen, 1987b). First we confirmed that the factor structure and loading patterns of the items used in assessing family integration, self-derogation, and transgression proneness were the same in the two groups.

The test of our hypotheses started with those effects that were assumed to be equal in both groups: the impact of income loss on family integration and the effect of self-derogation on transgression proneness. This restricted structural model already yielded an acceptable fit to the data ($\chi^2 = 220.01$, $df = 181$, $p = .025$). Thus hypotheses 1 and 4 were confirmed.

Subsequently, we checked whether the model could be further improved by taking into account those paths that were expected for highly sensitive adolescents only: the influence of family integration and income loss on self-derogation. As predicted according to the second hypothesis, the model can be significantly improved if self-derogation is assumed to be influenced by family integration ($\delta \chi^2 = 8.14$, $df = 1$, $p < .01$). Adolescents high in sensitivity to evaluation by significant others are indeed more vulnerable to strained family relations. There was no support for the third hypothesis; income loss had no direct effect on self-derogation.

Figure 3 presents the final result, showing the path model for adolescents high in sensitivity to significant others in the upper part and the corresponding model for less sensitive adolescents in the lower part. As can be seen, our expectations are largely met by the data. Family integration is positively influenced by stable income in both groups, but its impact on self-derogation appears only among adolescents high in sensitivity to significant others. Self-derogation, in turn, affects transgression proneness in both groups.

Figure 3. Effects of Economic Deprivation on Family Integration, Adolescents' Self-Derogation, and Transgression Proneness Among Adolescents with High and Low Sensitivity to Evaluation by Significant Others

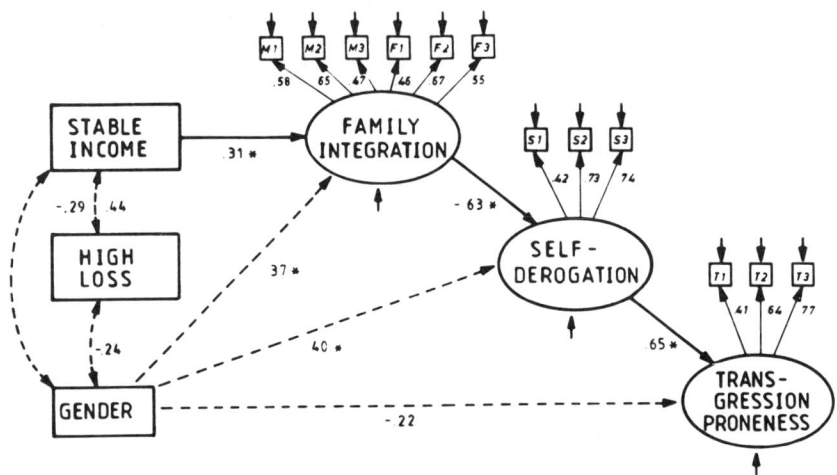

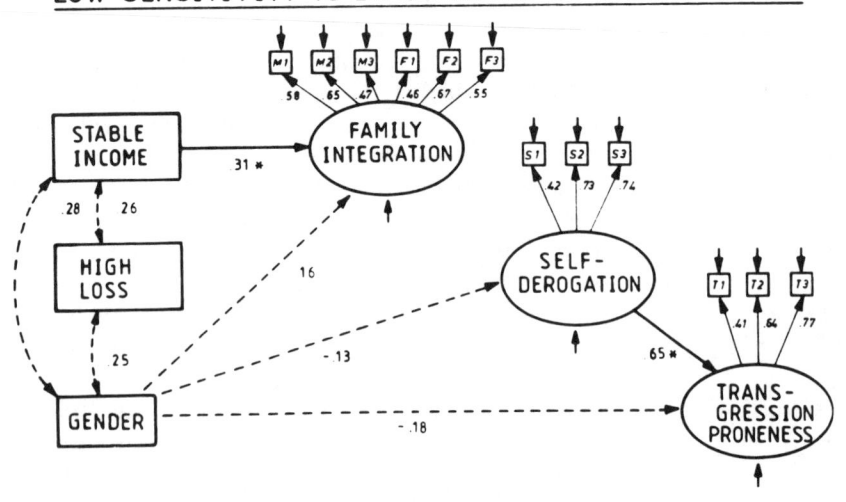

Note: Two-group LISREL analysis, loadings of multiple indicators, and standardized regression coefficients are given.

$^+p < .10$; $^*p < .05$; $^{**}p < .01$; $^{***}p < .001$.

The analyses in Studies 1, 2, and 3 were restricted to data from a selected sample of largely underprivileged families. Thus the generalizability of the results reported so far can be challenged. In the following study, we used a larger, more representative group of families that was not selected on the basis of income loss. Furthermore, we employed a longitudinal approach in order to control for initial differences among the adolescents.

Study 4: Further Evidence from Longitudinal Data

Instead of viewing sensitivity to evaluation by significant others as moderating the relation between economic loss and self-derogation, this study considers sensitivity to others (peers in particular) as the mediating link between financial hardship and family integration and between adolescents' self-derogation and transgression proneness.

An increased focus on peer relationships among adolescents experiencing economic deprivation was noted by Elder (1974; Elder, Van Nguyen, and Caspi, 1985). Two factors related to financial hardship may have contributed to this finding. First, as reductions in family income restrict adolescents' access to age-specific symbols of prestige (for example, expensive, fashionable clothing), their status among peers may become uncertain. Adolescents may develop higher sensitivity to evaluation by peers so that they are prepared to cope with discrepancies between aspirations and perceived performance. Second, parents' economic failure, and related family friction and lack of parental support, may affect parents' functioning as role models, motivating adolescents' search for alternative reference groups. A tendency among deprived youth to withdraw from adults and to engage in peer-group activities was observed in several studies conducted during the Great Depression (for example, Jahoda, Lazarsfeld, and Zeisel, 1975).

Because heightened awareness of one's image among peers facilitates the processing of negative self-related information, it can be expected to result in higher self-derogation (Duval and Wicklund, 1972). Impaired self-esteem, in turn, was already shown to be associated with increased transgression proneness in our studies reported above. Furthermore, as peers become a more important reference system during early adolescent development, susceptibility to contranormative peer influence seems to increase (Steinberg and Silverberg, 1986). Thus sensitivity to peer evaluation may also be related to transgression proneness. However, this effect should be mediated by adolescents' self-derogation.

In sum, several pathways are suggested to connect economic hardship to transgression proneness. First, economic loss leads to impaired family integration, which increases adolescents' focus on evaluations concerning the self provided by friends and classmates. This contributes to higher self-derogation, which, in turn, provides the mediating link to transgression proneness. Second, economic loss may directly influence adolescents' sensitivity to peers. Third, other direct links—between sensitivity to evaluation by others and transgression proneness, for example— are not expected. Rather, sensitivity and self-derogation are viewed as fully mediating the effects of change in income and family integration.

Sample. The sample consists of 458 two-parent families and their adolescent children who participated in the second (1983–1984) and third (1984–1985) waves of the Berlin Youth Longitudinal Study. Of these, forty-four families experienced a loss in income of more than 5 percent during the year prior to the parental assessment; twenty-two families (4.8 percent of the entire sample) reported a loss of more than 25 percent; and twenty-two families (4.8 percent) experienced a loss between 5 and 25 percent of their previous income. Families with gains in income were excluded in order to keep the design comparable to our previous analyses. Adolescents' median age at Time 1 was 13.2 years, ranging from eleven to seventeen years. Both sexes were equally represented. Parental data (including information on income loss) were gathered in the spring and adolescent data in the fall before and after the parent assessments.

Measures. Data on income loss were assessed as in the previous studies. Family integration was measured by mothers' reports only, using the same four items as in Study 1 (α = .72). Fathers' reports were not included since this would have further reduced the number of deprived families with complete data sets. Sensitivity to evaluation by significant others was assessed by three of the four items previously used, omitting the item related to parents (α at Time 1 and 2 = .71 and .75). Self-derogation was assessed by the same four items as in Study 2 (α at Time 1 and 2 = .70 and .68). The scale on transgression proneness includes one additional item that was not available at the earlier wave (α of this four-item scale at Time 1 and 2 = .68 and .73). Four-point ratings of agreement, ranging from 0 ("not at all") to 3 ("yes, very much"), were used as the response format.

Results. The means, standard deviations, and correlations of all variables are shown in Tables 1 and 2. A series of LISREL analyses was carried out. They provide an elegant way of testing the hypothesized mediation effects by systematically comparing models. Adolescent's age and gender as well as mother's education (highest school track or final degree accomplished, score ranging from 1 to 4) were included in all computations. Due to the longitudinal approach, all Time 2 effects concerning sensitivity to peer evaluation, self-derogation, and transgression proneness are independent of Time 1 influence.

Although the model as originally proposed provided an acceptable solution, it seemed reasonable to introduce minor changes in order to utilize more of the information given in the data. In addition to their mediating influence through self-derogation, both family integration and

Table 1. Correlations, Means, and Standard Deviations

Variable	2	3	4	M	SD
Income loss	-.14[a]	.01	.03	0.14	0.46
Parental education		-.04	-.17[b]	2.49	0.78
Adolescent gender			-.01	0.48	0.50
Adolescent age				13.18	1.64

[a] $p < .01$.
[b] $p < .001$.

Table 2. Time 1 and Time 2 Measures: Correlations, Means, and Standard Deviations

Variable	1	2	3	4	5	6	7
Family integration		.02	-.12[b]	-.05	-.09	-.10[b]	-.20[b]
Sensitivity to peers (Time 1)			.54[d]	.28[d]	.20[d]	.14[c]	18[d]
Sensitivity to peers (Time 2)				.16[c]	.21[d]	.13[c]	.21[d]
Self-derogation (Time 1)					.52[d]	.25[d]	.20[d]
Self-derogation (Time 2)						.16[c]	.24[d]
Transgression (Time 1)							.59[d]
Transgression (Time 2)							
Income loss	-.12[c]	-.01	.07	.06	.09[b]	.04	.10[b]
Parental education	-.03	.03	.13[c]	-.16[c]	-.12[b]	-.05	.01
Adolescent gender	.02	.06	.06	.09[b]	.09[a]	-.09[a]	-.16[c]
Adolescent age	.06	-.02	-.01	-.05	-.13[c]	.16[c]	.04
M	2.11	1.93	1.90	1.12	0.97	1.17	1.06
SD	0.60	0.70	0.70	0.59	0.56	0.65	0.67

[a] $p < .10$.
[b] $p < .05$.
[c] $p < .01$.
[d] $p < .001$.

sensitivity to evaluation by significant others were found to have a direct impact on transgression proneness. On the other hand, no direct effect of income loss on sensitivity to peer evaluations could be substantiated.

Figure 4 shows the ultimate path model omitting nonsignificant effects ($p > .05$). Bearing in mind the large sample size, this model yields an acceptable fit to the data ($\chi^2 = 52.06$, $df = 32$, $p = .014$; goodness-of-fit index = .98) as additionally indicated by a ratio χ^2 to df of less than 2 (see Bentler and Bonett, 1980). The effects of parental education and adolescent's age and gender are not shown in the figure. Briefly, self-

42 ECONOMIC STRESS: EFFECTS ON FAMILY LIFE AND CHILD DEVELOPMENT

Figure 4. LISREL Model for Effects of Family
Income Loss on Adolescents' Transgression Proneness
as Mediated Through Family Integration, Sensitivity to Evaluations
Peers, and Self-Derogation ($n = 458$)

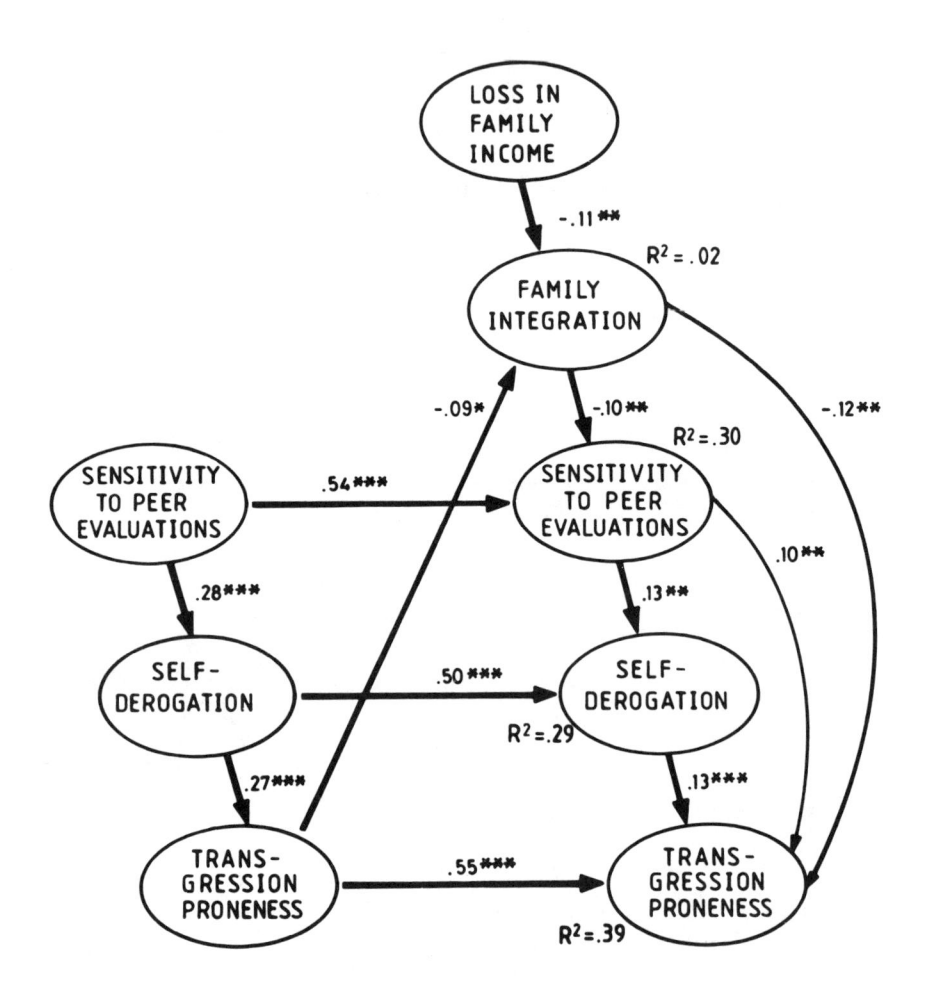

Note: Standardized regression coefficients (controlled for parental education and adolescents' age and gender) are shown.

$^{+}p < .10$; $^{*}p < .05$; $^{**}p < .01$; $^{***}p < .001$.

derogation is inversely related to mother's educational level and transgression proneness is higher among older adolescents and boys. As expected, income loss has a negative impact on family integration, which, in turn, contributes to adolescents' increased sensitivity to evaluation by peers. Such increased sensitivity to evaluation by peers indeed corresponds to higher self-derogation, which raises transgression proneness.

The direct effect of family integration on transgression proneness was not predicted. The association between both variables is also indicated by the path from adolescent's earlier transgression proneness to family integration. This may point to reciprocal cross-lagged effects, but conclusive evidence would require repeated measurements of family integration as well. In addition to the proposed mediating influence, sensitivity to evaluation by others also shows a direct effect on transgression proneness.

Hence, in trying to understand how financial hardship contributes to adolescents' transgression proneness, strained family relationships and subsequent changes in adolescents' sensitivity to peers seem to provide a better explanation than impaired self-esteem. Self-derogation seems to be only slightly affected by family integration and, hence, does not qualify as a mediator of these family characteristics. This conclusion from our present findings is not in line with the results of our previous analyses, which showed that the effects of family integration on transgression proneness were mediated through self-derogation.

We must keep in mind, however, that our earlier studies focused on particular risk groups using a small, underprivileged part of the original sample gathered in 1982. Furthermore, the children were two years younger. Thus an age-related decrease in the impact of the overall quality of family relations on adolescents' self-evaluation may also account for the discrepancy.

Conclusion

The Berlin Youth Longitudinal Study was not specifically designed to address issues of economic hardship. As in Elder's work, the advantage is that we can study the impact of economic change within the framework of normal development during adolescence. This advantage comes at a price. First, the number of families that were hit by severe economic hardship is necessarily small. Thus whenever a further breakdown of the sample would be useful, we run the risk of unreliable effects due to small sample sizes. Second, the measures we used had to be short in order to allow the assessment of many aspects of family functioning and personality development. Consequently, we are not quite satisfied with the psychometric quality and conceptual breadth of some of the instruments we derived. Third, partly because of restrictions in terms of sample size and partly because of the age range studied, we could not analyze the impact of economic hardship as a function of the adolescent's age.

Nevertheless, we were able to demonstrate the differential impact of economic hardship, depending on personal and contextual resources. The link to transgression proneness was observed irrespective of using the matched-group or the longitudinal design. Whether increased transgression proneness implies risks for later development, and if so for whom, still remains to be studied. Results from the 1930s suggest that in the long term some deprived adolescents may even profit—if the hard times provide opportunities to take responsibility and gain control over their development.

References

Anderson, R. N. "Rural Plant Closures: The Coping Behavior of Filipinos in Hawaii." *Family Relations*, 1980, *29*, 511-516.

Angell, R. C. *The Family Encounters the Depression*. Gloucester, Mass.: Peter Smith, 1936.

Bakke, E. W. *Citizens Without Work*. Hamden, Conn.: Archon Books, 1969. (Originally published 1940.)

Bentler, P. M., and Bonett, D. G. "Significance Tests and Goodness of Fit in the Analysis of Covariance Structures." *Psychological Bulletin*, 1980, *88*, 588-606.

Blyth, D. A., Simmons, R. G., and Carlton-Ford, S. "The Adjustment of Early Adolescents to School Transitions." *Journal of Early Adolescence*, 1983, *3*, 105-120.

Breuer, H., Schoor-Theisen, I., and Silbereisen, R. K. *Auswirkungen der Arbeitslosigkeit auf die Betroffenen Familien, Literaturstudie im Auftrag des Bündesministeriums für Jügend, Familie und Gesundheit* [Effects of employment on families. Study under the order of the Ministry of Youth, Family, and Health]. Bonn, W. Germany: H. Breur, I. Schoor-Theisen, and R. K. Silbereisen, 1984.

Cavan, R. C., and Ranck, K. H. *The Family and the Depression*. New York: Books for Libraries Press, 1969. (Originally published 1938.)

Cohen, J., and Cohen, P. *Applied Multiple Regression/Correlation Analysis for the Behavioral Sciences*. New York: Wiley, 1975.

Cooper, J. E., Holman, J., and Braithwaite, V. A. "Self-Esteem and Family Cohesion: The Child's Perspective and Adjustment." *Journal of Marriage and the Family*, 1983, *45*, 153-159.

Duval, S., and Wicklund, R. A. *A Theory of Objective Self-Awareness*. New York: Academic Press, 1972.

Elder, G. H., Jr. *Children of the Great Depression: Social Change in Life Experience*. Chicago: University of Chicago Press, 1974.

Elder, G. H., Jr., Caspi, A., and Downey, G. "Problem Behavior and Family Relationships: Life Course and Intergenerational Themes." In A. Sorensen, F. Weinert, and L. Sherrod (eds.), *Human Development and the Life Course: Multidisciplinary Perspectives*. Hillsdale, N.J.: Erlbaum, 1984.

Elder, G. H., Jr., Caspi, A., and Van Nguyen, T. "Resourceful and Vulnerable Children: Family Influences in Stressful Times." In R. K. Silbereisen and K. Eyferth (eds.), *Development as Action in Context*. New York: Springer, 1986.

Elder, G. H., Jr., Liker, J. K., and Cross, C. E. "Parent-Child Behavior in the Great Depression: Life Course and Inter-Generational Influences." In P. B. Baltes and G. O. Brim (eds.), *Life-Span Development and Behavior.* Vol. 6. New York: Academic Press, 1984.

Elder, G. H., Jr., Van Nguyen, T., and Caspi, A. "Linking Family Hardship to Children's Lives." *Child Development,* 1985, 56, 361-375.

Fenigstein, A., Scheier, M. F., and Buss, A. H. "Public and Private Self-Consciousness: Assessment and Theory." *Journal of Consulting and Clinical Psychology,* 1975, 43, 522-527.

Galambos, N. L., and Silbereisen, R. K. "Income Change, Parental Life Outlook, and Adolescent Expectation for Job Success." *Journal of Marriage and the Family,* 1987, 49, 141-149.

Heinelt, H., Wacker, A., and Welzer, H. "Arbeitslosigkeit in den 70er und 80er Jahren—Beschäftigungskrise und ihre Sozialen Folgen" [Unemployment in the 70s and 80s—employment crises and their social consequences]. *Archiv für Sozialgeschichte,* 1987, 27, 259-317.

Hetzer, H. *Kindheit und Armut.* Leipzig, E. Germany: Hirsel, 1929.

Jahoda, M., Lazarsfeld, P. F., and Zeisel, H. *Die Arbeitslosen von Marienthal: Ein Soziographischer Versuch* [The unemployed of Marienthal: a sociological approach]. Frankfurt, W. Germany: Suhrkamp, 1975. (Originally published 1933.)

Jöreskog, K. G., and Sörbom, D. *LISREL VI: Analysis of Linear Structural Relationships by Maximum Likelihood, Instrumental Variables, and Least Square Methods.* Mooresville, Ind.: Scientific Software, 1984.

Kaplan, H. B. *Deviant Behavior in Defense of Self.* New York: Academic Press, 1980.

Kessler, R. C. "Stress, Social Status, and Psychological Distress." *Journal of Health and Social Behavior,* 1979, 20, 259-272.

Larson, J. H. "The Effects of Husband's Unemployment on Marital and Family Relations in Blue-Collar Families." *Family Relations,* 1984, 33, 503-511.

Liem, R., and Liem, J. "Social Class and Mental Illness Reconsidered: The Role of Economic Status and Social Support." *Journal of Health and Social Behavior,* 1978, 19, 139-156.

Liker, J. K., and Elder, G. H., Jr., "Economic Hardship and Marital Relations in the 1930s." *American Sociological Review,* 1983, 48, 343-359.

McCarty, J. D., and Hoge, D. R. "The Dynamic of Self-Esteem and Delinquency." *American Journal of Sociology,* 1984, 90, 396-410.

Moos, R. H. *Family Environment Scale (FES): Preliminary Manual.* Palo Alto, Calif.: Social Ecology Laboratory, Department of Psychiatry, Stanford University, 1974.

Nunally, J. C. *Psychometric Theory.* New York: McGraw-Hill, 1967.

Scarr, S. "The Sorry State of Child Care in America." *International Society for the Study of Behavioural Development Newsletter,* 1989.

Schindler, H., and Wetzels, P. "Subjektive Bedeutung Familiärer Arbeitslosigkeit bei Schülern in einem Bremer Arbeiterstadtteil" [Subjective meaning of family unemployment on students in a blue-collar neighborhood of Bremen]. In T. Kieselbach and A. Wacker (eds.), *Individuelle und Gesellschaftliche Kosten der Massenarbeitslosigkeit: Psychologische Theorie und Praxis* [Individual and public costs of mass unemployment: psychological theory and practice]. Weinheim, W. Germany: Beltz, 1985.

Silbereisen, R. K., Reitzler, M., and Zank, S. "Stability and Change in Self-

Concept in Adolescence: Self-Knowledge and Self-Strategies." In F. Klix and H. Hagendorf (eds.), *Human Memory and Cognitive Capabilities: Mechanisms and Performance*. Symposium in Memoriam Hermann Ebbinghaus, Berlin, Humboldt University. Amsterdam: North-Holland, 1986.

Statistisches Bundesamt. *Statistisches Jahrbuch 1988* [Statistics yearbook 1988]. Stuttgart, W. Germany: Kohlhammer, 1988.

Steinberg, L., and Silverberg, S. B. "The Vicissitudes of Autonomy in Early Adolescence." *Child Development*, 1986, 57, 841-851.

Verdonik, F., and Sherrod, L. R. *An Inventory of Longitudinal Research on Childhood and Adolescence*. New York: Social Science Council, 1984.

Walper, S. *Familiäre Konsequenzen Ökonomischer Deprivation* [Family consequences of economic deprivation]. Munich, W. Germany: Psychologie Verlags Union, 1988.

Walper, S., and Silbereisen, R. K. "Familiäre Konsequenzen Ökonomischer Einbussen und ihre Auswirkungen auf die Bereitschaft zu Normverletzendem Verhalten bei Jugendlichen" [Family consequences of economic loss and their effects on tendencies toward delinquency among young people]. *Zeitschrift für Entwicklungspsychologie und Pädagogische Psychologie* [Journal of developmental and pedagogical psychology], 1987a, *19*, 228-248.

Walper, S., and Silbereisen, R. K. "Personal and Contextual Risk Factors in Coping with Economic Hardship." Paper presented at the ninth biennial meeting of the International Society for the Study of Behavioural Development, Tokyo, July 12-26, 1987b.

Zank, S. *Zur Entwicklung des Lösungsmittelschnuffelns bei Jugendlichen und Jungen Erwachsenen* [The development of volatile substance abuse by young people and young adults]. West Berlin: Berlin Verlag, 1988.

Rainer K. Silbereisen is professor of developmental psychology at the University of Giessen, Federal Republic of Germany. He is principal investigator of the Berlin Youth Longitudinal Study, a cross-cultural investigation into the relationship between problem behavior and normal youth development.

Sabine Walper is senior research scientist at the State Institute of Early Education and Family Research in Munich, Federal Republic of Germany. She is involved in longitudinal studies on adolescent development and early childhood in the family context.

Helfried T. Albrecht is research scientist at the University of Giessen, Federal Republic of Germany. He is involved in longitudinal analyses of control beliefs in the development of juvenile problem behavior.

Economic hardship diminishes psychological well-being and the capacity for supportive parenting. Single mothers' coping behavior, psychological functioning, and communications to the child about financial matters and personal problems predict the degree of psychological distress experienced by their children.

Maternal Behavior, Social Support, and Economic Conditions as Predictors of Distress in Children

Vonnie C. McLoyd, Leon Wilson

The link between economic hardship and diminished psychological well-being among adults is well established. Adults who are poor or have sustained major economic loss experience more mental health problems than their economically advantaged counterparts (McLoyd, 1989; McLoyd, in press). The increased presence of a range of frustrating life events and conditions outside the person's control, a hallmark of economic hardship, appears to be a major etiological factor underlying the link between economic hardship and mental health problems (Liem and Liem, 1978). Individuals who are poor, for example, are confronted with an unremitting succession of negative life events (eviction, physical illness, criminal assault) in the context of chronically stressful, ongoing

---

The research reported in this chapter was supported in part by a Faculty Scholar Award in Child Mental Health from the William T. Grant Foundation and a postdoctoral fellowship from the Rockefeller Foundation, both awarded to Vonnie McLoyd. During the preparation of this chapter, Leon Wilson was supported by a Rodney-DuBois-Mandela postdoctoral fellowship from the Center for Afro-American and African Studies at the University of Michigan. Portions of this research were presented in an invited symposium at the biennial meetings of the Society for Research in Child Development in Kansas City, April 1989. We thank the families who participated in the study and the staffs of the Michigan Department of Social Services and the Ypsilanti, Michigan, public schools for their cooperation and gratefully acknowledge the assistance of Liese Hull, Shannon Nelson, Patty Rich, and Eve Trager in data collection and coding.

life conditions such as inadequate housing and dangerous neighborhoods, which, together, markedly increase the exigencies of day-to-day existence. Because of limited financial resources, negative life events often precipitate additional crises so that stressors are highly contagious (Makosky, 1982).

Parents' mental health has far-reaching implications for their child-rearing behavior. A growing body of data, most of it from mothers of infants and children in preschool or early primary school, directly ties parental punitiveness, inconsistency, and unresponsiveness to negative emotional states in the parent. For example, an investigation by Conger and others (1984) indicated that black and white mothers who reported higher levels of emotional distress exhibited less positive behavior (for example, hugs and praise) and more negative behavior (for example, threats and derogatory statements) toward their children . Similarly, in a study of poor black and white mothers of five- to seven-year-olds, Longfellow, Zelkowitz, and Saunders (1982) found that the more highly stressed and depressed the mothers were, the less responsive they were to their children's dependency needs and the more hostile and dominating they were when initiating behavior toward the child and responding to the child's requests. Highly depressed mothers shouted and hit the child more frequently and relied less on reasoning and loss of privileges in disciplining their children than mothers who reported lower levels of depression. Considerably less is known about how psychological distress relates to the child-rearing behavior of parents of older children. In the study reported in this chapter, we examine the relations among economic hardship, maternal mental health, and parental behavior of black and nonblack single mothers whose children were in their preadolescent and adolescent years.

Economic Hardship, Parenting, and Children's Mental Health

Like their parents, children who are economically deprived are at high risk of suffering mental health problems. Social maladaptation and psychological problems such as depression, low self-confidence, peer conflict, and conduct disorders are more prevalent among poor children than among economically advantaged children (Gibbs, 1986; Kellam, Ensminger, and Turner, 1977; Langner and others, 1969, 1970; Levinson, 1969; Myers and King, 1983). Similarly, children of parents who have experienced job loss, severe income loss, or extended periods of unemployment are more likely to be depressed, lonely, withdrawn, and emotionally sensitive than children of parents with stable work and financial histories (Buss and Redburn, 1983; Elder, Van Nguyen, and Caspi, 1985; Lempers, Clark-Lempers, and Simons, 1989). They also are at higher risk for low self-esteem and behavior problems (Coopersmith, 1967; Flanagan, 1988; Isralowitz and Singer, 1986; Werner and Smith, 1982).

Although psychological problems are more prevalent among children experiencing economic hardship, compared to their economically advantaged counterparts, there is considerable variation in psychological functioning among economically deprived children. A major goal of our research was to identify some of the factors that account for this variation. We gave special attention to the mother's behavior. In particular, we examined the effects on children's psychological functioning of the following factors: maternal nurturance, maternal psychological functioning, the degree to which mothers discussed financial matters and personal problems with their children, and the extent to which mothers coped with economic hardship by attempting to generate income and curtail family consumption.

Recent studies provide direct evidence that at least some of the psychological and behavioral problems of children in families experiencing economic loss are mediated by punitive and harsh parental discipline brought on by economic hardship. Elder's pioneering studies of families of the Great Depression indicate that fathers who sustained heavy financial loss became more irritable, tense, and explosive, which, in turn, increased their tendency to be punitive and inconsistent in the discipline of their children. This behavior was predictive of temper tantrums, irritability, and negativism in young children, especially boys, and moodiness, hypersensitivity, feelings of inadequacy, and lowered aspirations in adolescent girls (Elder, 1979; Elder, Liker, and Cross, 1984; Elder, Van Nguyen, and Caspi, 1985). The parental behavior of mothers was not influenced by economic hardship.

The causal pathway documented by Elder linking economic loss to children's development through the father's behavior has been replicated in recent studies of contemporary children. In a study by Lempers, Clark-Lempers, and Simons (1989) of working-class and middle-class rural adolescents, for example, economic loss was linked to higher rates of adolescent delinquency and drug use due to an increase in inconsistent and punitive discipline by parents, as reported by the adolescents. It has also been shown that transgression proneness is higher among children living in families that have experienced economic loss than children in families that have experienced economic gain, but only when parental acceptance of the child is low (Galambos and Silbereisen, 1987). Other research is consistent with this mediational model, although it does not focus on fathers or economic hardship in particular. Patterson's programmatic research, for example, has demonstrated convincingly that stressful experiences increase psychological distress in mothers and produce changes in family and child management practices. Distressed mothers' increased use of aversive, coercive discipline, in turn, contributes to antisocial behavior in boys (Patterson, 1988; Patterson, DeBarsyshe, and Ramsey, 1989).

McLoyd (in press) hypothesizes that a similar mediational process operates within the context of poverty. For two reasons, however, she cautions against concluding that negative parental behavior is the primary pathway through which poverty undermines children's socioemotional functioning. First, supporting evidence is sparse. Second, the multifaceted nature of poverty, especially if it is chronic, appears to require more complex models of causality. Like parents who have suffered economic loss, parents living in poverty are at high risk of psychological distress. Single mothers constitute a group of particular concern—first because their prospects of poverty are greatly increased compared with married mothers and, second, because they are at greater risk of anxiety, depression, and health problems than other marital status groups. This risk is intensified if they are poor and live alone with their children (Garfinkel and McLanahan, 1986; Guttentag, Salasin, and Belle, 1980). Because they are more emotionally distressed than more affluent mothers, it is not surprising that poor mothers have been found to be less supportive, nurturant, and involved with their children (McLoyd, in press). We believe that this may partially account for the link between poverty and psychological impairment found among children. Research has shown consistently that children whose parents are nonsupportive have lower self-esteem and more psychological disorders, exhibit more antisocial behavior and behavioral problems (Coopersmith, 1967; Gecas, 1979; Rollins and Thomas, 1979), and are more likely to show arrested ego development (Powers, Hauser, and Kilner, 1989). These findings, as well as research indicating that children are adversely affected by economic loss when it results in punitive and inconsistent discipline, led us to expect that low maternal nurturance would be predictive of impaired psychological functioning among children in our study.

Children are highly sensitive to their parents' emotional state. When nondepressed mothers simulate depression, for example, their infants become distressed and make efforts to restore the mother's normal mood (Cohn and Tronick, 1983). Elder (1974) found that adolescent children whose fathers suffered major economic loss were more likely than children of nondeprived fathers to wish that "father were happier." In Longfellow, Zelkowitz, and Saunders' (1982) study of low-income families, children of stressed or depressed mothers were less likely to view their family life as happy, when compared to children whose mothers were less stressed or depressed. Infants and young children of depressed mothers behave in ways similar to their mothers. These children smile and express happiness less often and are more irritable and fussy than children of nondepressed mothers, perhaps reflecting a tendency of children to imitate negative affect modeled by their mothers (Downey and Coyne, forthcoming).

These findings suggest that in addition to negative parenting, economically disadvantaged parents may influence the socioemotional functioning of their children through a more passive mode. Specifically, the despondency and despair these parents model and the gloomy climate they establish in the home may foster melancholy in the child. Parents communicate the meaning of events and circumstances to their children by their affect and behavior and, in turn, instruct children about how to respond to particular situations (Bandura, 1977). Hence, deterioration in the parent's psychological functioning in the context of economic loss or poverty may become a communicable social phenomenon to the extent that the child imitates the symptomatic affect and behavior of the parent (Kelley, Sheldon, and Fox, 1985). Indeed, unemployed parents generally recognize that their reaction to the crisis of unemployment may serve as a model for the response of their children and worry that their children will sense their depression and anxiety about finances and the future (Elder, 1974; Cunningham, 1983). The possibility that children will model depressive affect may be heightened in single-parent families because these children lack the advantage of an additional parent or other resident adult who may temper a depressive outlook with a more optimistic and affectively positive style of coping (Brenner, 1984). In view of these considerations, we hypothesized that anxiety and depressive symptoms among single mothers would be predictive of greater psychological distress among children. We also expected that psychological distress would be greater among children whose mothers more frequently discussed their personal worries and financial matters with their children.

Another dimension of maternal functioning examined in our study is the strategies mothers adopt to ease economic hardship. We were particularly interested in whether the mother coped with economic hardship by making specific attempts to generate income or reduce family spending and the relation of these coping efforts to her psychological functioning and that of the child. A number of studies have examined whether particular styles of coping in the context of economic hardship are associated with more positive psychological functioning among adults. For example, Rosen (1983) found that working-class, unemployed women who made more cuts in family spending following their loss of employment suffered significantly higher psychological distress and demoralization compared to women who made fewer cuts. Similarly, the findings of a recent study of rural, middle-class families experiencing economic loss indicate that fathers in families that made more substantial economic adjustments to make ends meet experienced greater psychological distress (Elder, Conger, and Foster, 1989).

While the link between coping strategies and adults' psychological well-being has been established, extremely little is known about how children are affected by adaptations to economic hardship. Greater adaptations in the form of income generation and reduction of expenditures may undermine the child's psychological well-being directly or through their impact on the parent's affect and behavior toward the child. Alternatively, adaptation marked by specific problem-solving behavior intended to ease economic hardship, compared with more palliative forms of coping, may foster family unity and a sense of efficacy in the child that may, in turn, contribute to positive psychological functioning. In a study reported by Elder, Conger, and Foster (1989), family economic adjustments had no direct effect on the child's emotional state or the father's affect toward the child. Rather, adaptations to hardship aggravated men's irritability and hostility toward their wives and this led to hostility toward the child. In short, fathers displaced their anger toward the mother to the child. Our investigation examines the links between coping behavior and psychological functioning among children and, as such, provides additional data on this neglected issue.

Socioemotional Functioning and Children's Support Networks

Conflicting findings have been reported regarding the effects of social support on children's competence and socioemotional well-being. There is considerable evidence that support fosters psychological adjustment and protects children from the negative effects of stressful experiences (Sandler, Miller, Short, and Wolchik, 1989). Social support discriminates between resilient youth and youth with serious coping problems (Werner and Smith, 1982), moderates the relationship between stress and maladjustment in poor inner-city children (Sandler, 1980), and buffers the negative impact of parental divorce (Sandler and others, 1989) and school transitions (Berndt, 1989; Felner, Ginter, and Primavera, 1982).

Support from both peers and adults can benefit children under stress. For example, perceived emotional support from friends and the number of reciprocated best friends contributed independently to school competence, peer competence, and perceived self-competence in Cauce's (1986) sample of black, lower-class adolescents. In Williams and Kornblum's (1985) ethnographic study of poor, black urban children, positive adult role models who demonstrated interest in the children and shielded them from the more pernicious aspects of economically depressed neighborhoods figured prominently in the lives of the "superkids," that is, those children who were functioning well socioemotionally and educationally. Similarly, all of the high-risk but resilient individuals in Werner and Smith's (1982) well-known study of children of Kauai, at various points in their development, recruited a mentor to help them meet life's challenges. Many of these children had very early memories of a special adult who fostered confidence in their ability to succeed in spite of obstacles

(William T. Grant Foundation Commission on Work, Family, and Citizenship, 1988).

Support provided in the context of an enduring social bond appears to have more power to buffer the effects of stress. Riley and Cochran (1987) found evidence that both kinship status and gender of the supporter influenced the effect of support on young children. The school performance of sons of single mothers increased with an increase in the number of adult male relatives who took the child on outings away from home, but it was unrelated to the frequency of outings with female relatives or nonkin.

In other studies, however, social support is reported to be negatively related to psychological functioning. Higher levels of informal support (friends, nonfamilial adults) have been linked with lower academic adjustment among lower-class, nonwhite adolescents attending inner-city schools (Cauce, Felner, and Primavera, 1982; Felner, Aber, Primavera, and Cauce, 1985). Furthermore, family support was negatively related to the academic self-concept, general self-concept, and total self-concept of these adolescents (Cauce, Felner, and Primavera, 1982). In a similar vein, Hirsch and Reischl (1985), in a study of children of depressed parents, found that those who had stronger friendships and received more social support in relation to their most difficult family and school problem were more poorly adjusted than those who had weaker friendships and received less social support. Treadwell and Johnson's (1980) study of adolescents from diverse racial and socioeconomic backgrounds found no evidence that social support buffered the effects of negative life changes. Irrespective of the level of support received by the adolescents, negative life change related positively to various indicators of psychological and physical distress.

Discrepancies in research findings have fostered an appreciation for the multidimensionality of social support and the fact that the salience of social support as a mediator of positive adjustment depends on both the dimension of social support examined and the area of adjustment considered (Felner, Aber, Primavera, and Cauce, 1985). In the study reported here, we assess the contribution to children's psychological functioning of three dimensions of their support networks as reported by the children: number of peer and adult relatives and nonrelatives in the network, diversity of support (that is, the number of different kinds of support provided by each individual in the network), and perceived quality of interaction between the child and network members. We expected that fewer adult relatives and nonrelatives in the child's support network, less diversity in the kinds of support provided by individual members of the network, and lower perceived quality of support would be predictive of higher levels of psychological distress. We also examine the relation of psychological functioning to a number of demographic variables (child's age, sex, race) and quality of life indicators (degree of economic hardship, receipt of welfare assistance, number of negative life events).

Description of Research

The participants of the study were 155 children and their mothers, all of whom were single. Eighty-one (53 percent) of the women were separated or divorced, fifty-six (36 percent) had never been married, thirteen (8 percent) were living with a partner, and four (3 percent) were widowed. All children in the study resided with their mothers. The children ranged in age from nine to seventeen with a mean age of fourteen. Eighty-five (54.8 percent) were female and seventy (45.2 percent) were male. Eighty-five (54.8 percent) of the children were African American, sixty-two (40 percent) were Anglo-American, six (3.9 percent) were Asian American, and two (1.3 percent) were Hispanic American. Ninety-five (61.3 percent) of the families were receiving public welfare assistance in the form of Aid to Families with Dependent Children (mean income = $6,482 per year), while the remaining sixty women were primarily lower and working class (mean income = $16,354 per year). The women ranged in age from twenty-five to fifty-eight with a mean age of 35. Participants lived in a small midwestern city and were recruited through the Department of Social Services and a local school.

Each single mother who responded to a letter soliciting her participation in the study was contacted for the purpose of scheduling an interview with her and the child. Two research assistants went to the participant's home; one interviewed the mother and the other interviewed the child. The interviews were conducted in separate rooms.

Children's Psychological Functioning. Birleson's Self-Rating Scale of Depression, an eighteen-item scale, assessed the presence of several symptoms of *depression* including appetite disturbance, feelings of loneliness, and reduction in activity level. The child indicated whether or not each item applied to him or her most of the time (score of 2), sometimes (1), or never (0). *Anxiety* was assessed with the "What I Think and Feel" Scale, a revision of the Children's Manifest Anxiety Scale. It is a thirty-seven-item yes/no questionnaire with three factors, including physiological manifestations of anxiety (such as sweaty hands), worry and hypersensitivity, and fear and difficulty concentrating. Selected items from the Hopkins Symptom Checklist were used to assess *somatization*. The child indicated on a five-point scale how often he or she had had each of seventeen problems or complaints (such as headaches and nervousness) during the past thirty days (1 = not at all; 5 = a great deal). The scores on these three measures were highly correlated. Therefore, the scales were combined to constitute a single indicator of the child's psychological well-being. The internal consistency of this composite measure was acceptable (α = .75).

Mother's Psychological Functioning. *Depression* was measured with the Center for Epidemiological Studies Depression Scale (CES-D), which consists of twenty items representing the major components of the depressive syndrome: depressed mood, feelings of guilt and worthlessness, helplessness, and changes in eating and sleeping patterns. The mother indicated on a four-point scale how frequently she experienced these symptoms during the past week (1 = rarely or none of the time; 4 = most of the time). *Anxiety/somatization* was assessed with the anxiety and somatization scales of the Hopkins Symptom Checklist. Each mother indicated on a five-point scale how often she had each of twenty-one problems and complaints (such as headaches, nervousness, mind going blank) during the past thirty days (1 = not at all; 5 = a great deal). Because scores on the two measures were highly correlated, the scales were combined to constitute a single indicator of the mother's mental health (α = .73).

Maternal Behavior. To assess the salience of *nurturant versus punitive* parenting behavior, mothers were asked to indicate on a five-point scale how often they used nine different methods to punish and reward their children (such as verbal compliment, show of affection, scolding, taking away privileges). Based on a factor analysis, scores for these items were combined into two additive scales of nurturance and punitiveness. The final measure was the difference of the total scores for the two scales (nurturance minus punitiveness). Higher scores, therefore, indicate a greater tendency toward nurturant behavior. Mothers indicated on a frequency scale how often they shared their worries, discussed personal problems, and discussed the family's financial situation with the child. This three-item scale was used as an indicator of *maternal communication about problems* (α = .71). *Maternal adaptation to economic stress* was based on the mother's response (1 = yes; 0 = no) to a seventeen-item scale about things she had done in the past three months to reduce family expenditures (such as moved in with another adult to share rent, eaten out at restaurants or fast food places less often) or generate income (such as pawned household or personal items). Scores were computed by adding the number of coping behaviors reported by each mother.

Dimensions of the Child's Support Network. Using the Children's Inventory of Social Support developed by Wolchik, Sandler, and Braver, five kinds of support were identified: recreation/play; advice/information; services/goods (for example, help with homework or taking the child someplace); emotional support (for example, listening to the child when he or she is sad or afraid); and positive feedback (for example, telling the child something good about himself or herself). *Network size* was assessed by having children list all the people inside (relatives) and outside (nonrelatives) their families who had provided each kind of support during the previous two months. For each supporter, the child indicated whether the person was an adult or a child. As an indicator of *perceived quality of* *support,* the child rated how he or she felt about the time spent with each supporter (7 = "terrific"; 1 = "OK, not really good or bad"). A measure of the *diversity of support* was derived by assessing the number of different kinds of support each person in the network provided to the child.

Negative Life Events. Information about the occurrence of negative life changes experienced by the child within the past twelve months was gathered in a fifty-five-item inventory (yes/no format) administered to the mother. The core of this inventory consists of Coddington's Stressful Life Events Inventory for Children. In the analyses that follow, we include only those events that are negative or undesirable (such as child being a victim of violence, death of a family member or friend of the child). Our analytic variable, therefore, is the total number of negative life changes experienced by the child (maximum score = 53).

Demographic Variables. We considered the following demographic indicators in our analyses: *ethnicity* of the child (1 = nonblack; 0 = black); *sex* of the child (1 = female; 0 = male); *age* of the child, which was collapsed into five categories (12 years or less; 12.1 to 13 years; 13.1 to 14 years; 14.1 to 15 years; over 15 years); *AFDC status* (1 = yes; 0 = no); annual per capita *income;* and *degree of economic hardship,* based on the mother's response to three questions: "How difficult is it for you to meet the monthly payments on your family's bills?"; "In general, how do your family's finances usually work out at the end of the month? Do you find that you usually end up with some money left over, just enough to make ends meet, or not enough money to make ends meet?"; and "In the past three months, how often have you decided not to buy something you had been planning to purchase for yourself or for your children?" (α = .66). Higher scores indicate greater economic hardship.

Results

We present the results for three sets of analyses. First we discuss the factors we consider to be important antecedents and outcomes of maternal psychological functioning. This provides an important link in our later analysis of the impact of maternal functioning on children's psychological well-being. The second set of analyses is the bivariate relationship of various predictors of psychological distress in children. Finally, we use ordinary least squares regression (OLS) to model the multivariate relationship of several of these predictors of children's distress.

Economic Hardship, Adaptation, and Maternal Functioning. Our data confirmed a very significant link between the degree of economic hardship and mothers' psychological well-being. The positive coefficient (r = .34, p < .001) indicates that mothers experiencing greater economic hardship reported much higher levels of psychological distress than those who had fewer economic difficulties. As is to be expected, per capita income was negatively associated with psychological distress in the mother ($r = -.21$, $p < .02$). AFDC status did not significantly differentiate levels of psychological distress. Mothers under more economic strain also tended to make more efforts to generate income or reduce family expenditure ($r = .66$, $p < .001$). The most frequent ways in which mothers attempted to make ends meet were by cutting back on their social or recreation activities (63.6 percent), buying cheaper clothes for themselves (61 percent), purchasing cheaper food (55.8 percent), buying cheaper clothes for their children (48 percent), postponing a trip or vacation (46.8 percent), and reducing the use of household utilities (42.9 percent). Sixty-five percent of the women did not have savings from which they could draw; of those who did, 45 percent indicated that they had used between 25 and 100 percent of their savings in the past three months to make ends meet. The more efforts the mothers made to balance family needs and family income, the more distressed they were ($r = .34$, $p < .001$). We also found that mothers experiencing greater economic hardship discussed personal and financial problems a lot more with their children than mothers whose economic situation was more favorable ($r = .20$, $p < .01$).

Maternal Functioning and Parenting. The mental health status of the mothers in our study was also related to their parental behavior. Mothers experiencing more negative emotional states perceived their parenting roles as more difficult ($r = .33$, $p < .001$) than mothers reporting less psychological distress. Highly distressed mothers were also significantly less nurturant of their children ($r = -.22$, $p < .01$) and more communicative of their problems ($r = .17$, $p < .05$) than their counterparts with fewer psychological problems. Not surprisingly, mothers who found their maternal roles more stressful were less nurturant ($r = -.22$, $p < .01$) and discussed money matters and personal problems more frequently with their children ($r = .20$, $p < .01$).

Maternal Functioning and Children's Psychological Well-Being. In the next level of analyses, we assessed the links of various aspects of maternal functioning to psychological distress in children. First, as we expected, our data indicate a significant association between the psychological status of mothers and that of their preadolescent and adolescent children. The positive coefficient ($r = .19$, $p < .05$) indicates higher levels of distress in the child with increases in the level of psychological distress reported by the mother. Also interesting was the fact that mothers who more frequently communicate their problems and discussed money had children with elevated levels of psychological distress, compared with children whose mothers communicated less. The statistical association of these two variables, however, is only marginally significant ($r = .16$, $p < .10$).

Neither the degree of nurturance nor the strategies adopted by mothers for coping with economic hardship significantly related to their children's mental health, at least from the bivariate results. However, the negative coefficients ($r = -.04$, $r = -.09$, respectively) suggest that mothers who are more nurturant and adopt active strategies for coping with economic difficulties tend to have children who report fewer psychological problems. Additionally, our data indicate no statistically significant *direct* link between levels of economic hardship, as reported by mothers, and children's psychological well-being.

Social Support and Children's Psychological Well-Being. Of the dimensions of social support we considered, both number of nonrelative adults in the child's network and diversity of support provided by individual members of the network are positively related to psychological distress in the child, although the latter relationship is of marginal statistical significance ($r = .22$, $p < .01$, $r = .15$, $p < .10$, respectively). These results are contrary to our expectations. In line with our prediction, however, greater satisfaction with the interpersonal contact with family members is marginally associated with lower levels of psychological distress in children ($r = -.15$, $p < .10$).

Negative Life Events and Children's Psychological Well-Being. As expected, a very significant relationship was found between negative life events and the psychological functioning of the children. The more negative life events reported during the past twelve months, the higher the level of psychological distress reported by the child ($r = .27$, $p < .006$).

Demographic Factors and Children's Psychological Functioning. None of the demographic variables used in the bivariate analyses is statistically significant at the .05 alpha level. The directions of the coefficients indicate that psychological distress is somewhat higher among girls compared with boys ($r = .05$), among white children compared with black children ($r = .10$), and among younger children compared with older children ($r = -.09$). Despite the marginal relationships observed for these demographic variables, they are considered essential for the specification of the multivariate model described below.

The economic indicators used in our study bear little relation to the children's mental health. AFDC status, degree of economic stress reported by the mothers, and per capita income fail to yield significant relationships with children's psychological well-being. Thus while these variables are significantly related to mothers' well-being, they seem to have no direct effect on the psychological functioning of their children.

A Multivariate Model of Children's Psychological Well-Being. In this final level of analyses, we fitted a model describing the relationship of several predictors to the psychological well-being of the children. Consistent with the bivariate analyses discussed above, we examined the predictability of four sets of factors: maternal functioning and behavior, the child's support network, negative life events, and demographic and economic factors.

For the most part, the variables used in these analyses are the ones described earlier. For statistical reasons, however, some variables were omitted from the final model. For the child's social network, we used four variables: size of the adult nonrelatives network, size of the peer network, diversity of support, and children's reported satisfaction with the quality of supportive interaction with relatives. The size of the child's adult relatives network was omitted because of multicollinearity problems.

Of the economic indicators available in our data, we used per capital income in the final model. This was done since another viable indicator of the economic environment of the children—namely, level of economic hardship as reported by the mother (discussed earlier)—was highly correlated with the coping behavior adopted by these mothers, thus creating multicollinearity problems for our model. Since mothers' coping behavior was crucial to our analyses, we used per capita income.

Together the predictors in the model account for approximately 22 percent of the variability in children's psychological well-being after adjusting for degrees of freedom. Our checks for violation of the assumptions of the regression model did not reveal any serious departures from these requirements. The regression coefficients for the predictors are presented in Table 1. Relations are considered very significant at or below the .05 alpha level, while those above the .05 level but at or below the .10 level are considered marginally significant.

Maternal Behavior and Functioning. Consistent with our bivariate finding, mothers' level of psychological distress significantly predicted the level of psychological distress in their children. The degree to which these mothers communicated about money problems and personal problems, as was true in the bivariate case, was marginally significant. The positive coefficients (.19 and .14, respectively) for the two variables indicate associations that are consistent with our predictions. Thus the more depressed and anxious the mother and the more she talked to her child about her personal problems and the family's financial situation, the higher the level of psychological distress reported by the child. Given that the other variables are in the model, these two variables account for about 5 percent of the variance explained.

Maternal adaptation to economic strain was the strongest predictor in the model, accounting for 6 percent of the variance. The beta coefficient (-.27) indicates a negative association such that greater efforts by the mother to reduce family consumption and generate income predicted lower levels of psychological distress in the child.

Dimensions of the Child's Support Network. Contrary to expectation, a greater number of nonfamily adults in the child's network and greater diversity in the type of support provided by individual network members predicted significantly higher levels of psychological distress in the child

Table 1. **Standardized Regression Coefficients for the Predictors of Psychological Distress in Children** ($n = 155$)

Predictor	Beta	Error
Maternal characteristics		
Psychological distress	.19[b]	.081
Communication of problems	.14[a]	.078
Coping behavior	-.27[c]	.081
Nurturance	-.04	.075
Child's support network		
Peer network size	.07	.076
No. of adult nonrelatives	.23[b]	.077
Network diversity	.20[b]	.076
Quality of support	-.15[c]	.076
Negative life events	.23[c]	.079
Economic and demographic		
Per capita income	.05	.077
Child's age	-.22[c]	.077
Child's ethnicity	.02	.077
Child's sex	.11	.075
Constant	10.40	3.67
R^2 (adjusted)	.22	

[a] $p < .10$.
[b] $p < .05$.
[c] $p < .01$.

($\beta = .23$ and .20, respectively). That is, children with more nonfamily adults in their network, as well as children whose network members individually provided greater diversity of support, reported higher levels of psychological distress. These two variables account for 8 percent of the variance in children's psychological functioning. Quality of support by family members was negatively related to psychological distress; children who reported greater satisfaction with the time spent with family members experienced less psychological distress ($\beta = -.15$). Although statistically significant, this variable accounts for only 2 percent of the variance in children's psychological functioning. No significant effect of the size of the children's peer network was found.

Negative Life Events. As in the bivariate analysis, more negative life changes were predictive of higher psychological distress among children ($\beta = .23$).

Demographic and Economic Factors. Of the demographic variables included in the model, only age had a significant effect on children's psychological well-being. The beta coefficient (.22) indicates that younger children reported more psychological distress than children who were older. The fact that age became very significant in the multivariate model suggests that its relationship to children's psychological well-being may be suppressed in the bivariate model. Neither the sex nor the ethnicity of the child was a significant predictor of psychological distress. Finally, the economic situation of the child's family, as measured by per capita income, was unrelated to psychological functioning in the child.

In summary, then, our model provides evidence linking certain aspects of maternal functioning to children's psychological well-being. Significant relationships were observed for the mother's psychological states and her coping behavior. Sharing her difficulties with the child appeared to increase the child's psychological distress. The size of the child's nonrelative adult network and the diversity of support provided by individual members of the network predicted higher levels of psychological distress in the child. Quality of support by relatives also related to psychological distress in the expected direction. Finally, except for the ages of the children, demographic and economic variables failed to explain variation in children's psychological well-being.

Discussion

Mothers in our study who reported more difficulty meeting their financial responsibilities had less positive mental health. This finding is consistent with evidence from numerous other studies. For example, Dressler (1985) reported that chronic economic stress (difficulty paying bills, worrying about money, not having enough money for health care) was the strongest predictor of depression in blacks living in randomly selected households. Among the low-income mothers studied by Makosky (1982), income and money problems (for example, unpredictability and insecurity) were correlated but not interchangeable variables. Both income and money problems were strongly correlated with the mother's mental health; but even when income was controlled, money problems were significantly related to mental health.

The mothers in our study who were experiencing more acute economic hardship reported greater curtailment in spending and consumption and increased efforts to generate income. Coping behavior of this kind was associated with higher levels of psychological distress among mothers, a finding that is consistent with those reported by Rosen (1983) in her study of blue-collar women who lost jobs and by Elder, Conger, and Foster (1989) in their study of primarily middle-class families in rural Iowa. Women in our study, more often than not, had no savings. Hence their efforts to make ends meet often involved particularly painful, demoralizing cutbacks in day-to-day consumption. Moreover, when cutbacks were necessary it appears that mothers, rather than children, bore a disproportionate share of the burden of sacrifice, perhaps to attenuate feelings of deprivation in their children. One plausible interpretation of our data is that higher levels of anxiety and depression were the psychological costs of these sacrifices by the mother. Our data are correlational, however, and hence provide no basis for inferring a causal link between adaptations and psychological distress.

Unlike the families in our study, middle-class families often cope with economic loss or difficulty initially by drawing upon savings, liquidating major assets, and using credit more often (Elder, Conger, and Foster, 1989). Such resources stave off disruptions in the day-to-day, customary patterns of consumption and protect the essentials for living. Essentially, their first line of defense against economic loss is more likely to involve adjustments somewhat removed from daily functioning. As economic strain continues, adjustments are likely to increasingly affect the most mundane of daily activities such as use of household utilities, food habits, and transportation. Such adjustments can seriously undermine psychological well-being. The positive associations between economic hardship and adaptation, and between adaptation and psychological distress, probably explain, in part, why researchers find less psychological distress among middle-class men (compared with working-class men) and white men (compared with black men) who have lost jobs. That is, middle-class men and white men tend to have more financial resources than lower-status and black men. Consequently, when they suffer loss of employment or economic difficulty, their financial resources buffer the impact and adaptations are likely to be less extensive than those exacted from lower-status and black men.

While efforts to curtail consumption and increase income were positively associated with psychological distress among mothers, they were negatively associated with psychological distress among children. The latter relation may be mediated by the child's perception of the mother. Perhaps mothers who adopt a more active, problem-solving stance vis-à-vis economic strain, while more depressed and anxious themselves, are more likely to be perceived by their children as competent and concerned than mothers who adopt more palliative forms of coping. This may, in turn, engender a sense of efficacy and psychological security in the child. This is an important issue that deserves further study.

Our findings also indicate that the frequency with which mothers talked to their children about personal problems and financial matters predicted higher levels of psychological distress in children. This is reminiscent of Weiss's (1979) analysis of the echelon structure characterizing some single-parent households and his findings concerning the effects of certain echelon structures on children. He argues that in order to reduce role strain, single parents often encourage children to assume the role of partner rather than that of a subordinate member of the household. Compared with children in two-parent households, children in single-parent households generally do more household tasks and are more involved in household management and decision making. Moreover, because they see their children as bearing a fairly major responsibility for the functioning of the household, single parents often share their worries and problems with their children. In Weiss's study, adolescents who assumed the role of friend and confidant to their mothers came to have the same worries as their mothers. In particular, many of the adolescents were acutely aware that their parents were hard pressed for money and this appeared to cause anxiety and insecurity in some of them. Hence while the demands of single-parent households may foster maturity and feelings of competence and self-worth, they also may undermine children's psychological well-being, especially among those whose dependency needs are greater.

While the level of economic hardship was unrelated to the child's psychological functioning, it was positively related to psychological distress in the mother. Psychological distress in the mother was positively related to psychological problems in the child. This pattern of findings is consistent with evidence suggesting that economic hardship, rather than having direct effects, adversely affects children's socioemotional functioning in part through its impact on the parent. A number of investigations of this issue have specifically pointed to the parent's use of inconsistent and arbitrary discipline (Elder, Van Nguyen, and Caspi, 1985; McLoyd, in press). We conducted a series of path analyses to determine whether the link found in our study between mothers' and children's psychological functioning was mediated by life events, maternal nurturance, adaptations to economic hardship, or maternal communications about money matters and personal problems. None of these factors accounted for the relationship. Further work is needed to identify the intervening processes linking the psychological functioning of single mothers and their children.

Older adolescents reported less psychological distress than did younger adolescents. Perhaps younger adolescents have less mature coping strategies, are less effective in marshaling psychological resources needed to attenuate distress, and have a greater tendency to cognitively appraise negative experiences as threatening. Furthermore, younger adolescents typically have less social freedom than older adolescents. Consequently, their exposure to negative experiences in the home may be greater.

Our findings present a mixed picture of the relation between children's psychological functioning and various dimensions of their support network. Social networks marked by more satisfying contact with family members were associated with lower psychological distress in the child. However, supportive relations with an increased number of adult nonrelatives and greater variety in the type of support each individual provided were associated with higher psychological distress in the child. These two findings may reflect a tendency of adolescents experiencing more mental health problems to seek more support from others outside the family (for example, teachers). This may also explain the negative relation between psychological support and adjustment reported by other researchers (Cauce, Felner, and Primavera, 1982; Hirsch and Reischl, 1985). Another possibility is that the support provided by adult nonrelatives to the children in our study actually threatened, rather than enhanced, children's self-esteem. This, in turn, may have produced more rather than less psychological distress. There is evidence that supportive acts perceived by the recipients to enhance their self-esteem are positively linked to self-esteem, whereas supportive acts that elicit negative self-cognitions are positively linked to self-deprecation, anxiety, and depression (Sandler and others, 1989). These findings, along with the pattern of findings in our study, emphasize the need to understand the conditions under which supportive relationships either facilitate or undermine children's psychological functioning. In short, as Sandler and others (1989) have observed, much more attention needs to be given to the intervening processes by which support affects children's adjustment.

References

Bandura, A. *Social Learning Theory.* Englewood Cliffs, N.J.: Prentice-Hall, 1977.

Berndt, T. "Obtaining Support from Friends During Childhood and Adolescence." In D. Belle (ed.), *Children's Social Networks and Social Supports.* New York: Wiley, 1989.

Brenner, A. *Helping Children Cope with Stress.* Lexington, Mass.: Heath, 1984.

Buss, T., and Redburn, F. S. *Mass Unemployment: Plant Closings and Community Mental Health.* Newbury Park, Calif.: Sage, 1983.

Cauce, A. M. "Social Networks and Social Competence: Exploring the Effects of Early Adolescent Friendships." *American Journal of Community Psychology,* 1986, *14,* 609-628.

Cauce, A. M., Felner, R. D., and Primavera, J. "Social Support in High-Risk Adolescents: Structural Components and Adaptive Impact." *American Journal of Community Psychology,* 1982, *10,* 417-428.

Cohn, J., and Tronick, E. "Three-Month-Old Infants' Reactions to Simulated Maternal Depression." *Child Development,* 1983, *54,* 185-190.

Conger, R., McCarty, J., Yang, R., Lahey, B., and Kropp, J. "Perception of Child, Child-Rearing Values, and Emotional Distress as Mediating Links Between Environmental Stressors and Observed Maternal Behavior." *Child Development,* 1984, *54,* 2234-2243.

Coopersmith, S. *The Antecedents of Self-Esteem.* San Francisco: Freeman, 1967.

Cunningham, S. "Shock of Layoff Felt Deep Inside Family Circle." *American Psychological Association Monitor,* 1983, *14,* 10-14.

Downey, G., and Coyne, J. "Children of Depressed Parents: An Integrative Review." Forthcoming.

Dressler, W. "Extended Family Relationships, Social Support, and Mental Health in a Southern Black Community." *Journal of Health and Social Behavior,* 1985, *26,* 39-48.

Elder, G. *Children of the Great Depression.* Chicago: University of Chicago Press, 1974.

Elder, G. "Historical Change in Life Patterns and Personality." In P. Baltes and O. Brim (eds.), *Life Span Development and Behavior.* Vol. 2. New York: Academic Press, 1979.
Elder, G., Conger, R., and Foster, E. "Families Under Economic Pressure." Unpublished paper, University of North Carolina, 1989.
Elder, G., Liker, J., and Cross, C. "Parent-Child Behavior in the Great Depression: Life Course and Intergenerational Influences." In P. Baltes and O. Brim (eds.), *Life-Span Development and Behavior.* Vol. 6. Orlando, Fla.: Academic Press, 1984.
Elder, G., Van Nguyen, T., and Caspi, A. "Linking Family Hardship to Children's Lives." *Child Development,* 1985, *56,* 361–375.
Felner, R. D., Aber, M. S., Primavera, J., and Cauce, A. M. "Adaptation and Vulnerability in High-Risk Adolescents." *American Journal of Community Psychology,* 1985, *13,* 365–379.
Felner, R. D., Ginter, M., and Primavera, J. "Primary Prevention During School Transitions: Social Support and Environmental Structure." *American Journal of Community Psychology,* 1982, *10,* 277–290.
Flanagan, C. "Parents' Work Security and the Young Adolescent's Development." Unpublished manuscript, University of Michigan, 1988.
Galambos, N., and Silbereisen, R. "Influences of Income Change and Parental Acceptance on Adolescent Transgression Proneness and Peer Relations." *European Journal of Psychology of Education,* 1987, *1,* 17–28.
Garfinkel, I., and McLanahan, S. *Single Mothers and Their Children.* Washington, D.C.: Urban Institute, 1986.
Gecas, V. "The Influence of Social Class on Socialization." In W. Burr, R. Hill, F. Nye, and I. Reiss (eds.), *Contemporary Theories About the Family: Research-Based Theories.* New York: Free Press, 1979.
Gibbs, J. "Assessment of Depression in Urban Adolescent Females: Implications for Early Intervention Strategies." *American Journal of Social Psychiatry,* 1986, *6,* 50–56.
Guttentag, M., Salasin, S., and Belle, D. *The Mental Health of Women.* New York: Academic Press, 1980.
Hirsch, B. J., and Reischl, T. "Social Networks and Developmental Psychopathology: A Comparison of Adolescent Children of a Depressed, Arthritic, or Normal Parent." *Journal of Abnormal Psychology,* 1985, *94,* 272–281.
Isralowitz, R., and Singer, M. "Unemployment and Its Impact on Adolescent Work Values." *Adolescence,* 1986, *21,* 145–158.
Kellam, S., Ensminger, M. E., and Turner, R. "Family Structure and the Mental Health of Children." *Archives of General Psychiatry,* 1977, *34,* 1012–1022.
Kelley, R., Sheldon, A., and Fox, G. "The Impact of Economic Dislocation on the Health of Children." In J. Boulet, A. M. DeBritto, and S. A. Ray (eds.), *The Impact of Poverty and Unemployment on Children.* Ann Arbor: University of Michigan Bush Program in Child Development and Social Policy, 1985.
Langner, R., Greene, E., Herson, J., Jameson, J., Goff, J., Rostkowski, J., and Zykorie, D. "Psychiatric Impairment in Welfare and Non-Welfare Children." *Welfare in Review,* 1969, *7,* 10–21.
Lempers, J., Clark-Lempers, D., and Simons, R. "Economic Hardship, Parenting, and Distress in Adolescence." *Child Development,* 1989, *60,* 25–49.
Levinson, P. "The Next Generation: A Study of Children in AFDC Families." *Welfare in Review,* 1969, *7,* 1–9.
Liem, R., and Liem, J. "Social Class and Mental Illness Reconsidered: The

Role of Economic Stress and Social Support." *Journal of Mental Health and Social Behavior,* 1978, *19,* 139-156.

Longfellow, C., Zelkowitz, P., and Saunders, E. "The Quality of Mother-Child Relationships." In D. Belle (ed.), *Lives in Stress: Women and Depression.* Newbury Park, Calif.: Sage, 1982.

McLoyd, V. C. "Socialization and Development in a Changing Economy: The Effects of Paternal Job and Income Loss on Children." *American Psychologist,* 1989, *44,* 293-302.

McLoyd, V. C. "The Impact of Economic Hardship on Black Families and Children: Psychological Distress, Parenting, and Socioemotional Development." *Child Development,* in press.

Makosky, V. P. "Sources of Stress: Events or Conditions." In D. Belle (ed.), *Lives in Stress: Women and Depression.* Newbury Park, Calif.: Sage, 1982.

Myers, H. F., and King, L. "Mental Heath Issues in the Development of Black American Children." In G. Powell, J. Yamamoto, A. Romero, and A. Morales (eds.), *The Psychosocial Development of Minority Group Children.* New York: Brunner/Mazel, 1983.

Patterson, G. "Stress: A Change Agent for Family Process." In N. Garmezy and M. Rutter (eds.), *Stress, Coping and Development in Children.* Baltimore, Md.: Johns Hopkins University Press, 1988.

Patterson, G., DeBarsyshe, B., and Ramsey, E. "A Developmental Perspective on Antisocial Behavior." *American Psychologist,* 1989, *44,* 329-335.

Powers, S., Hauser, S., and Kilner, L. "Adolescent Mental Health." *American Psychologist,* 1989, *44,* 200-208.

Riley, D., and Cochran, M. "Children's Relationships with Nonparental Adults: Sex-Specific Connections to Early School Success." *Sex Roles,* 1987, *17,* 637-655.

Rollins, B., and Thomas, D. "Parental Support, Power, and Control Techniques in the Socialization of Children." In W. Burr, R. Hill, F. Nye, and I. Reiss (eds.), *Contemporary Theories About the Family: Research-Based Theories.* Vol. 1. New York: Free Press, 1979.

Rosen, E. "Laid Off: Displaced Blue Collar Women in New England." Paper presented at annual meeting of the Society for the Study of Social Problems, Detroit, September 1983.

Sandler, I. "Social Support Resources, Stress, and Maladjustment of Poor Children." *American Journal of Community Psychology,* 1980, *8,* 41-52.

Sandler, I., Miller, P., Short, J., and Wolchik, S. "Social Support as a Protective Factor for Children in Stress." In D. Belle (ed.), *Children's Social Networks and Social Supports.* New York: Wiley, 1989.

Treadwell, M., and Johnson, J. "Correlates of Adolescent Life Stress as Related to Race, SES, and Levels of Perceived Social Support." *Journal of Clinical Child Psychology,* 1980, *9,* 13-16.

Weiss, R. S. "Growing Up a Little Faster: The Experience of Growing Up in a Single-Parent Household." *Journal of Social Issues,* 1979, *4,* 97-111.

Werner, E., and Smith, R. *Vulnerable But Invincible: A Study of Resilient Children.* New York: McGraw-Hill, 1982.

William T. Grant Foundation Commission on Work, Family and Citizenship. *The Forgotten Half: Pathways to Success for America's Youth and Young Families.* Washington, D.C.: William T. Grant Foundation, 1988.

Williams, T., and Kornblum, W. *Growing Up Poor.* Lexington, Mass.: Lexington Books, 1985.

Vonnie C. McLoyd is an associate professor in the Department of Psychology and research associate in the Center for Human Growth and Development at the University of Michigan. She is the principal investigator of a longitudinal study of the impact of maternal job and income loss on African American children and their families, funded by the National Institute of Mental Health.

Leon Wilson is currently a Rodney-DuBois-Mandela postdoctoral fellow at the Center for Afro-American and African Studies, University of Michigan, where he conducts cross-cultural research on Caribbean and African American families.

Economic changes in the Farm Belt have undermined the security of life on the family farm. Rural adolescents are trying to come to terms with the meaning of the "farm crisis" for their identity and for their future.

The Iowa Farm Crisis: Perceptions, Interpretations, and Family Patterns

Mary P. Van Hook

The farm crisis of the 1980s created hardships in rural areas unparalleled since the Great Depression. Shock waves from these hardships affected individuals, families, and whole communities. Adolescents faced these difficulties at a critical stage of their lives, a time when they were still very much a part of their families although already beginning to plan their adult lives. Understanding how these economic problems affect rural youth and the ways in which they and their families cope with these disruptions can help us identify sources of stress and strength within rural families facing economic difficulties. To do so requires an analysis of the farm crisis itself and the cultural context in which rural families live.

Farm Crisis

Although rural areas have experienced a series of economic problems over the years, the term *farm crisis* specifically refers to a lengthy period of severe economic distress that began in the late 1970s in major agricultural portions of the United States. These economic difficulties had their source in a series of widespread economic and social events: shrinking international markets for agricultural products, monetary policies that halted the inflationary spiral, lending policies that rapidly escalated inter-

---

This study was funded by faculty research awards from the School of Social Work and the Horace H. Rackham School of Graduate Studies at the University of Michigan.

est rates while basing credit on markedly depreciated land values and cash flow, and prices for agricultural products that failed to meet the cost of production. These events culminated in more farm foreclosures and bank failures than at any time since the Great Depression, along with a substantial portion of other farmers who developed dangerous debt-to-asset ratios. Problems further reverberated throughout the rural communities with decreased sales, bad debts, major layoffs in agriculturally related industries, and a reduced ability to maintain community schools, churches, and service programs (Erb, 1985; Cochran, 1986; Perkins, 1985; Blair, 1986; Hines, Green, and Petrulis, 1986; Little, Prouix, Marlow, and Knaub, 1988). The impact on specific families in an area, however, varied widely. Especially hard hit were those who had just begun farming, those who had expanded their operations during the period of rapid inflation, and older farmers who had used their own operation as collateral to finance the entry of offspring into farming (Jolly, 1985).

While the farm economy in general has demonstrated recent signs of recovery, many family farms continue to be in a precarious financial position (Office of Technology Assessment, 1986). Parents of school-age children are at greatest risk for continued economic problems because they entered farming when prices for land, machinery, and credit were high and they currently hold the highest debt-to-asset ratios (Jolly, 1985).

Rural Community Context

Rural definitions of identity, stress, and acceptable resources can influence how these events are experienced. Rural residents experience their sense of personal well-being through participation in the social structure of the community. Stress is felt when their place in this social structure is jeopardized (Wilkening and McGranahan, 1978; Norem and Blundall, 1988). Identity is further derived from the family and its place within the community. The rural family serves as the central focus for both reproduction and production. Decisions made by the family regarding the allocation of its material or labor resources determine the family's survival as well as the position of members within the family unit and the community at large (Bokemeier and Garkovitch, 1987). Rural youth are highly socialized into the world of farming as a result of the visible nature of their parents' activities as well as their own active participation in this work. This participation also forms the basis for their own sense of personal competence and responsibility (Rosenblatt and Anderson, 1981).

Landownership for many rural families symbolizes family obligations toward the past and the future (Farmer, 1986; Salamon, 1980). Family members may thus experience an intense sense of loss when they can no longer retain the family farm or continue in farming (Halton, 1986; Ricchiardi, 1986; Heffernan and Heffernan, 1986; Farmer, 1986; *NASW*

News, May 1985; Florke and Kjenaas, 1984; Norem and Blundall, 1988). Values that emphasize the work ethic, autonomy, independence, and privacy can further increase stress and also make it difficult for residents to reach out to others with offers or requests for help (Kenkel, 1986; Wright and Rosenblatt, 1988).

Family issues influence the way in which stress is experienced by adolescents generally (D'Arcy and Siddique, 1984; Compas, Slavin, Wagner, and Vannatta, 1986; Burt, Cohen, and Bjorck, 1988). Efforts of family members in general to cope with difficulties are facilitated by family resources such as effective problem-solving strategies, supportive relationships, communication patterns, and ties with the social environment as well as an organizational system that involves a balanced degree of cohesion and adaptability (Billings and Moos, 1982; Smets and Hartup, 1988; D'Arcy and Siddique, 1984; Reiss, 1981; Conger and others, 1984; Walsh, 1982).

Impact on Families and Adolescents

The farm crisis has been a potential source of disruption for many rural families. Signs of this stress include increases in family tension and violence, reduced parental consistency, role strain arising from the need to take on additional and new types of responsibilities, and changes in the family balance of power (Norem and Blundall, 1988; Keating, Munro, and Doherty, 1988; National Action Commission on the Mental Health of Rural Americans, 1988). In adults this stress has been manifested primarily through depression, withdrawal from others, somatic symptoms, sleeping and eating disturbances, thoughts of worthlessness, mental confusion, rapid mood changes, and anxiety (Heffernan and Heffernan, 1986; Farmer, 1986, 1988a, 1988b; Policy Forum on Rural Stress, 1987; National Action Commission on the Mental Heath of Rural Americans, 1988).

Economic distress and the accompanying family tensions have contributed to increased levels of worry, depression, suicide attempts, loneliness, and pressure in rural adolescents (Cohen, 1987; Lempers, Clark-Lempers, and Simons, 1989; Joyce Walker, personal communication, August 10, 1988). Financial hardship has been associated with lower academic performance for junior high students, especially for boys who experienced reduced emotional support from their families (Clark-Lempers and Netusil, 1988). It also causes parents to be less nurturing and consistent, which, in turn, increases adolescents' depression and loneliness. When parents are inconsistent, their adolescents also tend to become involved in drug use and delinquency (Lempers, Clark-Lempers, and Simons, 1989). Clinical data suggest that some economically troubled rural youth have experienced burdensome guilt feelings (Van Hook, 1987). Rural youth tend to rely on close friends for support and contact other nonfamily members rarely and then only under conditions of great duress (Garfinkle, Hoberman, Parson, and Walker, 1988). Despite the problems cited above, most rural adolescents appear to be satisfied with their way of coping with stress and are optimistic about their own future (Cohen, 1987). Young people generally report that their family is experiencing less severe financial difficulties than their parents report. This suggests that parents may be protecting children from the full reality of family difficulties (Lempers, Clark-Lempers, and Simons, 1989; Clark-Lempers and Netusil, 1988). The farm crisis has accelerated the redirection of career goals away from agriculture and increased the value attributed to education (Sundberg, Tyler, and Poole, 1984; Kilman, 1988; Etchison, 1987).

In view of widespread evidence from survey and clinical data that the farm crisis has disrupted the lives of rural families and adolescents, a study was designed to obtain a qualitative picture from a nonclinical sample of rural adolescents. The study was designed to identify the meaning of this event for adolescents in terms of how they coped, their own role in the problem faced by the family, their future plans, and their view of the world.

Based on prior studies with rural families, it was hypothesized that adolescents would report that these economic disruptions had increased the stress experienced by themselves and adult family members. The nature of this stress would further be influenced by several aspects of rural families and communities. That is, the socialization patterns of rural youth described earlier would be likely to create a sense of responsibility to the family that would be manifest in a sense of guilt and in efforts to help the family. Family communication patterns, especially when combined with the complex nature of the farm crisis, would contribute to stress through increasing uncertainty. Supportive ties to the environment would be limited by family and community codes of independence and privacy as well as the selective nature of the farm crisis, which devastated some families and left others relatively unscathed. Adolescents would further attribute family survival to efforts that addressed the financial issues facing the family as well as the emotional needs of family members. The ability of family members to communicate with and support their adolescents would be important. The farm crisis was also likely to direct the career plans of rural youth away from agriculture.

Methodology

Sample. Adolescents were selected from two major agricultural counties in Iowa. Sioux County (the leading agricultural sales county in the state) and Guthrie County evidenced the disruptions typical of the farm crisis in terms of loss of property values and serious financial reverses of farmers and agriculturally related businesses. The sample was representative of the ethnic groups in these areas, primarily German, Dutch, and a mixture of other Northern European groups.

Participants were obtained from suggestions of school and Cooperative Extension staff, pastors, and other adolescent respondents as "youth who were likely to be knowledgeable about the impact of the farm crisis." Potential respondents and their parents were contacted by telephone in order to explain the nature of the study and to enlist their cooperation. This method had the danger of biasing the sample toward leaders and underrepresenting the more alienated. The response rate was high (80 percent). Several who declined to participate indicated that the interview would be too painful for them. Only data obtained from the forty-nine adolescents who had experienced either moderate or serious financial disruptions were included in the analysis. This information was supplemented by interviews with pastors, the Cooperative Extension staff, the county school guidance counselors, parents of seven of these adolescents, and four rural adolescents who had not experienced financial distress.

Adolescent respondents included twenty-four males and twenty-five females from two-parent households. The mean age of respondents was 16.8 years (SD = 1.24). The mean age of the parents was forty-five years (ranging from thirty-two to fifty-eight). For the most part, the primary or secondary occupation of the father had been in farming prior to the farm crisis. As is typical in many midwestern rural areas, these farms were generally major financial operations. Other family members were linked to the rural economy as owners of agriculturally related businesses, rural bankers, salesmen, and skilled laborers. The mothers' occupations varied widely. Thirty-five of the families (71.5 percent) had experienced major financial problems while another fourteen (28.5 percent) had experienced moderately severe problems.

Instrument. Between June 1987 and June 1988, adolescents participated in a semistructured interview in their homes. The interview was organized around the following basic areas: descriptions of the farm crisis; personal experiences and coping efforts (ways in which the farm crisis affected adolescents and their families, adolescent perceptions of the causes of their family problems, ways in which adolescents and their families coped with these problems, ways in which adolescents learned about family problems, adolescent reactions to this information, and how adolescents and others communicated about these problems with those outside the family); and long-term impacts of the farm crisis (lasting family changes created by the farm crisis and family efforts to cope with it and adolescent perceptions regarding the fairness of life, future plans, and roles of men and women). The General Health Questionnaire (GHQ version 28) was used to assess the general mental health of the adolescents. This series of questions regarding social and work activities, physical symptoms, and psychological distress is designed to reveal symptoms of depression, social dysfunction, somatization, and anxiety in the respondent. GHQ has been demonstrated to be a reliable scale for nonpsychotic distress, including anxiety ($\alpha = .87$), social dysfunction (.63), somatization (.65), and depression (.73) in populations with different characteristics, including adolescents (Goldberg and Hiller, 1970; D'Arcy and Siddique, 1984). Alpha coefficients for the study population were somewhat lower: anxiety, .65; social dysfunction, .63; somatization, .65; and depression, .73. Interviews were conducted by the author and two trained interviewers.

Data Analysis

Categories were developed to analyze the open-ended questions on the basis of a detailed content analysis of the responses of adolescents. The work of Pearlin and Schooler (1978) and Barbarin, Hughes, and Chesler (1985) was particularly influential in establishing the categories used for family coping. Family coping efforts were further analyzed in terms of the dimensions of family cohesion and flexibility. Cohesion was characterized by efforts that required the family to draw together either to solve the economic problems (for example, a son who gave his money to his family) or to maintain the emotional stability of family members (for example, sharing with other family members for support). Flexibility was evidenced by the adoption of new family roles within the family (for example, the wife who began working outside the family, the man who began doing dishes).

Data were analyzed to determine whether gender or birth order in the family (oldest, middle, youngest) or degree of economic difficulty (moderate, serious) was related to the way the farm crisis was experienced. Serious disruptions included loss of farm or business, bankruptcy, and other major business losses. Moderate disruptions referred to major reductions in the standard of living due to the farm and business problems. Degree of financial difficulty in this study referred to the financial problems experienced by the family at the time of the farm crisis, not currently.

Categorical data were analyzed by means of the chi square or the Fisher exact tests. The unpaired Student t test was used to analyze the impact of gender, economic difficulty, and coping strategies on the GHQ. Although generally only differences between groups that reached the $p < .05$ level of probability will be considered statistically significant, given the small sample represented here, trends of interest that did not reach this level are indicated with appropriate levels of probability. With the exception of the General Health Questionnaire, data in this study were obtained in response to open-ended questions. As a result, responses cited by at least 20 percent of the respondents were considered important enough to include in the following analyses.

Results

Adolescent Perceptions of the Impact of the Farm Crisis. When asked how the farm crisis affected their families, adolescents reported important instrumental and relationship changes.

Family Instrumental Changes. The most striking change involved the increased work responsibilities of their parents off the family farm or business (66 percent of the families). Fathers moved from farming to other types of work or supplemented the farm income with other work. A majority (63 percent) of adolescents reported that their mothers either began working off the farm or increased their hours in response to the farm crisis. This change in the mother's working meant increased responsibilities for the majority of adolescents involved. Female adolescents were more likely to experience this increase than were males (Fisher exact p = .03). While most adolescents took these changes in stride, approximately 20 percent reported that the mother's increased work prevented her from carrying out essential family responsibilities.

Family Relationship Changes. Family tensions increased in response to the economic uncertainties and change in family roles. With respect to the influence of gender on what adolescents perceived or at least reported, several weak trends emerged. Females were more likely than males to report an increase in family tensions (Fisher exact p = .06). Males, however, were more likely than females to report changes that reflected alterations in the balance between men and women in the family (Fisher exact p = .07). Change in balance meant that the mothers had gained greater power and respect within the family because of the income they provided. School personnel reported that there had been isolated instances of serious family problems and that younger children seemed more emotionally needy.

Adolescent Reactions. When asked about their own reactions to the farm crisis, adolescents indicated that it was an anxious time for them. They reported experiencing feelings of pressure (42 percent), helplessness (26 percent), and a variety of worries: losing the farm (43 percent), moving away from the area (39 percent), concern about the effect of these problems on their parents (24 percent), and social embarrassment (18 percent). Weak gender differences emerged in terms of the greater likelihood that males would be worried about the loss of the farm ($\chi_2(1)$ = 2.95, p < .07) and females would be worried about the effect on their parents ($\chi^2(1)$ = 3.18, p < .05). Adolescents expressed concern about their parents' emotional and physical health as a result of these problems. As one young person commented, "I can build a future off the farm for myself, but the farm has always been my parents' life." Oldest children in the family were also more likely than any others to be worried about the effect on their parents ($\chi^2(2)$ = 4.85, $p < .03$).

Behavioral responses of adolescents varied widely. In general, examples of problematic behavior were matched by others who made special efforts to be good and responsible. Some reported decreased school performance; others had markedly improved school performance. Guidance counselors confirmed these diverse patterns and also reported that adolescents were generally more concerned about their education and the future. Young people further indicated that expressions of pain tended to be muted and, therefore, not evident to others who did not fully understand the situation. Further information about adolescent responses will be analyzed here in terms of coping efforts.

Results on the General Health Questionnaire demonstrated considerable long-term resiliency by these adolescents. At the time of the interview, adolescents were generally experiencing symptoms on an occasional basis. On a scale of 1 = never, 2 = occasional (at least monthly), 3 = frequently (at least weekly), and 4 = daily, their scores were: general physical health (M = 1.61, SD = .34); anxiety (M = 1.69, SD = .39); apathy or lack of investment in activities (M = 1.9, SD = .32); and depression (M = 1.21, SD = .26). There were no significant differences based on either gender or the severity of the family's financial problems.

In evaluating these results and comparing them with other studies on the effect of economic distress on adolescents, it is important to keep in mind the timing of this study relative to the problems experienced by these families. Most adolescents had experienced the worst of the family difficulties during the years that characterized the worst of the farm crisis (1984–1986). They further indicated during the course of the interview that they had experienced more symptoms at that time than they were reporting currently.

Family and Community Information Networks. When asked how they learned about the problems of their own family or that of their friends, respondents described the presence of major gaps in the information systems of their families and the community at large. These gaps affected both how adolescents learned about the problem and the availability of support. In terms of the family, only half of the adolescents learned about the family problems directly from their parents. Other important sources of information included overhearing talk about the problem and drawing conclusions based on changes in spending habits. Although adolescents frequently indicated that lack of information increased their anxiety, none of them had asked their parents. Instead they used sibling networks of information. If families had a meeting to discuss the problem, it made an indelible impression on respondents. Meetings that were held several years ago were described with the immediacy and detail of a recent event. Although one can speculate that failure to ask for information might have served the purpose of denial for some respondents, the prevalence of these sibling networks suggests that family norms of discretion and protection of parents played a role. This protectiveness was particularly captured in the comment of one young woman: "It would have hurt my father much too much to have to tell me what was going on."

Adolescents described family and community codes of privacy that contributed to their isolation from others. Most of the adolescents had talked to no one outside the family (54 percent) or only with a few close friends (34 percent). Similar reports were given in terms of how people in the community at large shared information about problems due to the farm crisis. This code of privacy was substantiated by school staff and pastors. The selective nature of the farm crisis, which brought financial disaster to some families and left others unscathed, created additional barriers to communication. Respondents described a subtle screening process that was used to determine whether peers and adults could be trusted. Essential elements for establishing trust and credibility appeared to involve a personal understanding of the problem itself and demonstrated respect for the family of the adolescent.

These codes of family and community privacy, combined with the complex nature of the farm crisis itself, had the potential for increasing the insecurity of adolescents. In the words of one young woman: "One week your friends tell you that everything is fine, the next week you learn that their family's farm is up for sale. It is hard to know what is really going on and when you will be next." Although most young people were forewarned about problems within their own family, several reported being unaware of difficulties until the family had to give up the farm. This lack of preparation was epitomized in the comment of one young man: "I had no idea we were really in trouble until Dad said that we would have to sell the farm."

Communication barriers within the community also led to distortions regarding the true extent of the problem. For example, some financially untroubled youth were totally unaware of the existence of the serious problems experienced by their classmates in classes as small as thirty students.

Adolescent Interpretations of the Farm Crisis. When asked to describe what had caused the farm crisis, adolescents attributed it to a variety of external factors. Yet when asked if they had felt personally responsible for their family's economic problems, many (63 percent) indicated having experienced a sense of personal responsibility. Feelings of responsibility were not significantly related to either birth order or gender, although there was a tendency for females to feel more responsible than males ($\chi^2(1) = 2.86$, $p < .09$). Adolescents attributed their personal responsibility to beliefs that they had not worked hard enough or their parents had spent too much money on them because of special projects, their education, or health problems. Adolescents attempted to cope with these feelings of responsibility by trying harder to help, cutting back on their spending, or discussing things with their parents. Most adolescents had resolved their guilt feelings. Those who continued to feel guilty found it especially hard to talk with their parents.

Fairness of Life. When adolescents were asked if they felt that life was fair, 82 percent reported they felt it was unfair. The selective nature of the farm crisis contributed to the view that life is not fair. They reported that they felt it was unfair that their own parents had to work as hard or even harder than other people and yet were not rewarded for these efforts.

Adolescent Coping Efforts. When asked how they personally had tried to cope with the uncertainties and problems associated with the farm crisis, the majority (71 percent) reported that they had tried to help their family. The specific behavior involved in helping varied (for example, working harder, giving one's savings to the family, reducing spending, doing better in school, being available to listen to the parents). However, all adolescents perceived that these efforts represented a contribution to the family's welfare. Although information about the problem created the worries and anxiety discussed earlier, it was also described as helpful because it enabled adolescents to develop a plan of action. This response was typified by the comment of a young woman: "I was glad that I knew what was causing the tensions in the family because then I knew I could help by not asking my parents to buy me things and by getting a part-time job."

The two other major coping efforts of adolescents were staying away from home (36 percent) and staying home more (22 percent). Staying away from home was especially associated with increased family tensions ($\chi^2(1) = 5.2$, $p < .02$). Acceptance of the situation was also important for 63 percent of the respondents. Relying upon others outside the family unit for help played a minimal role for most of these adolescents.

Family Coping Efforts. When asked what their family had done to cope with the problems associated with the farm crisis, adolescents described a variety of efforts organized around solving the financial problems and meeting the emotional needs of the family members. While males and females generally reported similar coping efforts, males were more likely to report that their family had anticipated problems and had left farming (Fisher exact $p = .06$). This difference may reflect the greater tendency for rural families to expect male rather than female children to maintain the family farm or business. Adolescents attributed family survival to family cohesive effort (71 percent) and family flexibility (79 percent).

Associations between specific coping variables and differences in levels in the current mental and physical health status of adolescents were not statistically significant. There was a trend, however, that increased anxiety was associated with evidence of family flexibility ($t(1)$ = 1.87, p = .06). At the same time, family flexibility has been cited as a family resource in this study and others. It is difficult to ascertain whether anxiety was generated primarily by the changes in family roles or the presence of major disruptions that required these changes.

Adolescent Perceptions of Long-Term Family Changes. When asked what long-term effect their family's efforts to cope with the farm crisis had on the family, adolescents reported they made their family relationships more flexible (46 percent) and closer (33 percent). Efforts requiring the family to band together (cohesion) were associated with long-term closer family relationships ($\chi^2(1)$ = 6.4, $p < .01$). These adolescents reported that everyone in the family knew that they were needed during these difficult times. Respondents also indicated that the farm crisis had made their families more cautious about spending money (37 percent).

Adolescent View of Sex Roles. When asked how events associated with the farm crisis had affected their views regarding the roles of men and women, most adolescents reported that their view of sex roles had broadened. Changes within their own family, especially their mother's working more outside the home and family business as well as the increased importance of this work to the welfare of the family, particularly influenced this change. As one young adolescent male commented: "I began to realize that women could do more than laundry and cooking. They can do anything within their physical strength."

Adolescent Career Plans for the Future. In response to the question regarding the impact of the farm crisis on their own career plans for the future, adolescents reported that they had redirected their career goals away from farming and other agriculturally dependent businesses. The majority of adolescents thought that education was a ticket to security. The 16 percent of adolescents who wanted to be involved in agriculture in some way also planned to prepare themselves with education beyond high school. The low high school dropout rates in these communities (1 percent) indicate a context of community support for education. Adolescents who had shifted vocational plans away from agriculture generally reported parental approval of this change. Several young people expressed a fondness for their community but were convinced there were no vocational opportunities there. Females planned to get an education and vocational experience to protect themselves from the economic vulnerability experienced by many of their own mothers.

Discussion

The potentially disruptive effects of economic distress on rural adolescents and their families receive support from both survey and qualitative studies. The picture that emerges incorporates both pain and resiliency. Unfortunately, some characteristics of rural families that contributed to resiliency also had the potential for creating additional stress. The code of mutual family responsibility, evidenced in the efforts of adolescents to help and the ability of many families to band together to resolve their difficulties, carried with it the risk of adolescents bearing an unrealistic sense of responsibility for family problems. Families needed to be flexible enough to shift roles within the family in order to survive these difficult times. In many of these families, for example, economic survival depended on the mother's job outside the home or family business. In turn, other members had to assume additional family responsibilities. These same shifts, however, contributed to adolescent anxiety.

In view of the sense of helplessness experienced by adolescents, efforts to contribute to the family might also represent means by which they sought to gain mastery over their situation. These efforts can thus be potentially helpful both to the adolescents and to their families. At the emotional level, participating in the process of resolving family problems could contribute to the development of a sense of competence as a person. Although these adolescents assumed heavy burdens of responsibility and uncertainty for several years, they were finally able to participate in a process that resulted in some resolution of family difficulties. There appear to be similarities between these adolescents and those from middle-class families who experienced economic distress during the Great Depression. In Elder's (1974) classic study of the impact of the Great Depression on youth, adolescents from economically distressed middle-class families manifested greater ego strength as adults than did either youth from lower-class families or those from middle-class families who did not experience economic distress. This increased ego strength is attributed in part to a sense of personal competence created by the opportunity to assume additional responsibilities successfully.

The question is thus raised regarding the impact of long-term economic distress on rural adolescents—that is, what is the advantage of working hard and contributing to the family economy if it does not help; what kind of a person am I that my efforts do not help? Without the experience of success, will these adolescents experience greater demoralization and alienation? The high levels of depression and suicide attempts that have characterized adolescents from the Iron Mountain Range in Minnesota where long-term economic depression has persisted (Joyce Walker, personal communication, August 10, 1988) suggest greater potential danger for adolescents under these circumstances.

Family and community codes of protection, privacy, and independence may contribute to feelings of guilt and limit the ability of rural adolescents to draw upon the resources of other family members and the community at large. The work ethic remains an important orientation for rural adolescents despite their sense that life is not fair. Rather than alienation, a picture emerges of young people determined to prepare themselves to cope with an uncertain and unfair world. As farming has increasingly lost its credibility as a source of security, education has emerged as the primary means of ensuring some sense of security.

Participation in the complex and costly operations typical of contemporary midwestern farming may contribute to the development of a set of expectations as well as organization and planning skills that can be important resources in further education and other vocational areas. These circumstances provide rural youth with quite a different set of resources than those of young people from families where long-term poverty has been the pattern.

Despite the picture of long-term resiliency portrayed here, the increased levels of anxiety, depression, and suicide attempts reported among economically distressed rural adolescents continue to make this a high-risk population during difficult times. This is especially true because adolescents tend to respond to what is taking place currently in their lives. Counselors working with adolescents must further be aware that stress need not be manifested by the typical signs of pathology. It can also be manifested in behavior typically considered positive (for example, more responsible behavior and better school performance). In order to establish credibility with rural youth, counselors need to be informed about the reality of economic and social problems facing rural families and the meaning these events are likely to have for family members.

Rural adolescents appear to have considerable ability to assess their current situation and to develop career plans accordingly. They represent a major resource for rural areas that may well be lost unless successful community development efforts can convince the adolescents that a viable future is possible in this area. An exodus of young people from rural areas could create additional strains in the support systems for rural families.

Although the farm crisis was a source of distress for both sexes, some trends in gender differences emerged. The tendency for females to show greater concern for their parents and to assume more family responsibilities than males reflects traditional female socialization patterns. Males were more likely to be concerned about the future of the farm or business operation as well as changes in traditional family patterns.

With evidence that generally younger adolescents tend to be more vulnerable to family tensions than older adolescents (Smets and Hartup, 1988), further research is needed regarding the impact of economic distress on younger children (Clark-Lempers and Netusil, 1988). Younger children may lack some of the characteristics—such as mobility, growing independence from the family, increased ability to understand the nature of the problem and to create alternative plans, and somewhat better access to information—that enabled adolescents in this sample to cope as well as they did. The studies cited here depended on either retrospective qualitative data or survey information. Long-term observational data would be helpful in delineating the interaction between specific family variables, coping strategies, and the impact of economic stress on rural youth. A long-term study has recently been instituted in Iowa under the leadership of Rand Conger of Iowa State University that will provide useful information about these interactions. It is also important to examine the long-term effects on adolescents as they move into adulthood.

Despite the limitations of the studies cited, economic distress emerges as a potential source of pain for adolescents and their families. The nature of this pain and the resources that contribute to resiliency are shaped by the contemporary rural context.

References

Barbarin, O., Hughes, D., and Chesler, M. "Stress, Coping and Marital Functioning Among Parents of Children with Cancer." *Journal of Marriage and the Family*, 1985, *47* (2), 473-489.

Billings, A., and Moos, R. "Family Environments and Adaptation: A Clinically Applicable Typology." *American Journal of Family Therapy*, 1982, *10* (2), 26-35.

Blair, K. "More Iowans Now Seeking Help on Food." *Des Moines Register*, September 29, 1986, p. 1.

Bokemeier, J., and Garkovitch, L. "Assessing the Influence of Farm Wives' Self-Identity on Task Allocation and Decision Allocation." *Rural Sociology*, 1987, *52* (1), 13-76.

Burt, C., Cohen, L., and Bjorck, J. "Perceived Family Environment as a Moderator of Young Adolescents' Life Stress Adjustment." *American Journal of Community Psychology*, 1988, *16* (1), 101-122.

Clark-Lempers, D., and Netusil, A. "The Effects of Financial Stress on the Achievement of Young Adolescents from Farm and Nonfarm Families." Paper presented at annual meeting of the American Educational Research Association, New Orleans, April 1988.

Cochran, C. "Closings Mark a Grim Year for Banking." *Des Moines Register*, January 26, 1986, p. 12.

Cohen, J. "Spring 1987 Student Survey." Unpublished raw data. South Central Community Mental Health Center, Kearney, Nebraska, 1987.

Compas, B., Slavin, L., Wagner, B., and Vannatta, K. "Relationship of Life Events and Social Support with Psychological Dysfunction Among Adolescents." *Journal of Youth and Adolescence*, 1986, *15* (3), 205-221.

Conger, R., McCarty, J., Yang, R., Lahey, B., and Kropp, J. "Perception of Child, Child-Rearing Values, and Emotional Distress as Mediating Links Between Environmental Stressors and Observed Maternal Behavior." *Child Development*, 1984, *55* (5), 2234-2247.

D'Arcy, C., and Siddique, C. M. "Psychological Distress Among Canadian Adolescents." *Psychological Medicine*, 1984, *14* (3), 629-642.

Elder, G. *Children of the Great Depression*. Chicago: University of Chicago Press, 1974.

Erb, G. "Land Values Drop 17% Despite Positive Signs: Farmers' Key Assets Show a Loss of 63% Since 1981." *Des Moines Register,* August 12, 1985, p. 1.

Etchison, D. "The Impact of the Farm Crisis on Rural Adolescent Youth." Paper presented to the National Association for Rural Mental Health, Hendersonville, North Carolina, October 1987.

Farmer, V. "Broken Heartland." *Psychology Today,* 1986, *20* (4), 54–62.

Farmer, V. "Farm Crisis in the West." Paper presented to the National Association for Rural Mental Health, Billings, Montana, July 1988a.

Farmer, V. "South Dakota Rural Mental Health Needs Assessment." Paper presented to the National Association for Rural Mental Health, Billings, Montana, July 1988b.

Florke, B., and Kjenaas, M. "Distress and Dislocated Farm Families." Cherokee, Iowa: Mental Health Institute, 1984.

Garfinkle, B., Hoberman, H., Parson, J., and Walker, J. "Stress, Depression and Suicide: A Study of Adolescents in Minnesota." St. Paul: University of Minnesota, 1988.

Goldberg, D., and Hiller, V. F. "A Scaled Version of the General Health Questionnaire." *Psychological Medicine,* 1970, *9* (1), 139–145.

Halton, L. "In South Dakota, Old Autumn Ghosts." *New York Times,* November 1986, p. 1.

Heffernan, J., and Heffernan, W. "When Farmers Have to Give Up Farming." *Rural Development Perspectives,* 1986, *2* (3), 28–31.

Hines, F., Green, B., and Petrulis, M. "Vulnerability to Farm Problems Varies by Region." *Rural Development Perspectives,* 1986, *2* (3), 10–14.

Jolly, B. *Survey of Farm Operators.* Ames: Iowa State University Press, 1985.

Keating, N., Munro, B., and Doherty, M. "Psychosomatic Stress Among Farm Men and Women." In R. Marotz-Baden, C. Hennon, and T. Brubaker (eds.), *Families in Rural America: Stress, Adaptation, and Revitalization.* St. Paul, Minn.: National Council of Family Relations, 1988.

Kenkel, M. "Stress-Coping-Support in Rural Communities: A Model for Primary Prevention." *American Journal of Community Psychology,* 1986, *14* (5), 457–478.

Kilman, S. "Some Young People Go Back to the Land Despite Great Obstacles." *Wall Street Journal,* April 11, 1988, pp. 1–2.

Lempers, J., Clark-Lempers, D., and Simons, R. "Economic Hardships, Parenting, and Distress in Adolescence." *Child Development,* 1989, *60* (1), 25–39.

Little, L., Prouix, F., Marlow, J., and Knaub, P. "The History of Recent Farm Legislation: Implications for Farm Families." In R. Marotz-Baden, C. Hennon, and T. Brubaker (eds.), *Families in Rural America: Stress, Adaptation, and Revitalization.* St. Paul, Minn.: National Council of Family Relations, 1988.

National Action Commission on the Mental Health of Rural Americans. *Summary Report.* Alexandria, Va.: National Mental Health Association, 1988.

Norem, R., and Blundall, J. "Farm Families and Marital Disruptions During a Time of Crisis." In R. Marotz-Baden, C. Hennon, and T. Brubaker (eds.), *Families in Rural America: Stress, Adaptation, and Revitalization.* St. Paul, Minn.: National Council of Family Relations, 1988.

Office of Technology Assessment. *Technology, Public Policy, and the Changing Structure of American Agriculture.* Washington, D.C.: Government Printing Office, 1986.

Pearlin, L., and Schooler, C. "The Structure of Coping." *Journal of Health and Social Behavior,* 1978, *19,* 2–21.

Perkins, J. "Farm Debts Called Threat to Business." *Des Moines Register,* August 12, 1985, p. 1.

Policy Forum on Rural Stress. *Summary Report.* Rockville, Md.: National Institute of Mental Health, 1987.

Reiss, D. *The Family's Construction of Reality.* Cambridge, Mass.: Harvard University Press, 1981.

Ricchiardi, S. "Shattered Dreams." *Des Moines Register,* December 7, 1986, p. 1.

Rosenblatt, P., and Anderson, R. "Interaction in Farm Families: Tension and Stress." In R. Coward and W. Smith (eds.), *The Family in Rural Society.* Boulder, Colo.: Westview Press, 1981.

Salamon, S. "Farm Family Land Transfers." *Rural Sociology,* 1980, *45* (2), 290-308.

Smets, A., and Hartup, W. "Systems and Symptoms: Family Cohesion, Adaptability, and Childhood Behavior Problems." *Journal of Abnormal Childhood Behavior,* 1988, *16* (2), 233-246.

"Social Workers Aid Harried Farm Families." *National Association of Social Workers News,* May 1985, pp. 3, 5-6.

Sundberg, N., Tyler, L., and Poole, M. "Decade Differences in Rural Adolescents' View of Life Possibilities." *Journal of Youth and Adolescence,* 1984, *13* (1), 45-55.

Van Hook, M. "Harvest of Despair: Using the ABCX Model for Farm Families in Crisis." *Social Casework,* 1987, *68* (5), 273-279.

Walsh, F. *Normal Family Processes.* New York: Guilford Press, 1982.

Wilkening, E., and McGranahan, D. "Correlates of Subjective Wellbeing in Northern Wisconsin." *Social Indicators Research,* 1978, *5,* 211-234.

Wright, S., and Rosenblatt, P. "Isolation and Farm Loss: Why Neighbors May Not Be Supportive." In R. Marotz-Baden, C. Hennon, and T. Brubaker (eds.), *Families in Rural America: Stress, Adaptation, and Revitalization.* St. Paul, Minn.: National Council of Family Relations, 1988.

Mary P. Van Hook is an assistant professor at the University of Michigan School of Social Work. She was formerly the director of a mental health program in rural Iowa.

Because of chronic joblessness, the adolescent-to-adult transition is a special psychosocial challenge for black youth with far-reaching developmental implications.

The Adolescent-to-Adult Transition: Discouragement Among Jobless Black Youth

Phillip J. Bowman

The transition from adolescence to adulthood is a very challenging period, especially in technologically advanced urban societies. Because of unique difficulties faced during this period, psychologists have begun to recognize that adolescence often merges into a subsequent transitional stage known variously as "late adolescence," "youth," or "early adulthood" (Atwater, 1988; Keniston, 1970; Levinson and others, 1978). Bowman (1989) and others have noted that during this developmental transition, the salient role expectation shifts from "doing well in school" to "getting a job":

> This salient role shift is not only imposed by society, community, and family but is also personally reinforced as these social expectations are internalized into one's own value system. Hence, the work role becomes the major life arena for role strain processes [p. 129].

An earlier version of this chapter was presented as part of an invited symposium at the 1989 biennial meeting of the Society for Research on Child Development. Research for this chapter was undertaken with funding from the National Research Council and Ford Foundation.

The Bureau of Labor Statistics, a division of the U.S. Department of Labor, is the primary source of official government statistics on joblessness cited in this chapter. In addition to monthly statistical tabulations, I utilized a quarterly report on "Employment in Perspective: Minority Workers" and a 1982 report by the U.S. Commission on Civil Rights entitled "Unemployment and Underemployment Among Blacks, Hispanics, and Women."

Although meeting salient work-role expectations is often difficult for youth of all races, chronic joblessness has made the school-to-work transition a special psychosocial challenge for black youth (Bowman, 1984; Jones, 1989). The extreme difficulty in job search experienced by increasing numbers of black youth is nonnormative and has far-reaching developmental implications. Compared with whites, black youth enter the labor market earlier, are more often restricted by inadequate education, remain jobless for longer periods, experience greater frustration in their job search, and face more severe consequences from chronic job search difficulty throughout the adult life cycle (Adams and Mangum, 1978; Anderson and Sawhill, 1980; Bowman, 1989; Freeman and Wise, 1982).

The age range for the adolescent-to-adult transitional period may vary, but it usually includes any number of years between the ages of eighteen and thirty. For affluent American youth who attend college, the school-to-work transition is often delayed until as late as the early thirties when many with graduate and professional degrees enter the labor market for relatively permanent jobs. However, entry into the labor market more often occurs upon high school completion at about eighteen years of age. Among black youth, the transition from school to work is often initiated even earlier as many from low-income families seek jobs prior to completing high school in an effort to contribute to the family's economic subsistence (Bowman, 1988; Malveaux, 1989). Regardless of the specific age, chronic difficulties in job search make youth neither adolescents nor full-fledged adults.

Developmentally, it is important to understand the nature, antecedents, and consequences of chronic job search difficulty in the adolescent-to-adult transition. A prolonged transitional period has emerged out of necessity for more time to prepare for the skill demands of adult employment in a postindustrial, urban society that is rapidly changing. As in any society that requires a highly skilled labor force, educational preparation during the preadult years is a pivotal prerequisite for a successful transition from school to work in America (Bowman, in press; Wilson, 1978, 1987). In terms of consequences, failure to gain employment tends to preclude economic independence from one's family of origin and the ability to provide economically for the next generation. Therefore, finding gainful employment has crucial developmental consequences because it is not only the normative prerequisite for supporting oneself but also a pivotal precursor for achieving generativity and integrity during later adult stages (Bowman, 1989; Erikson, 1980).

Because black youth are at such high risk for chronic joblessness, this chapter highlights several issues related to their job search difficulties in the adolescent-to-adult transition. An important distinction is made between objective and subjective aspects of their chronic job search strain.

Emphasis is also placed on possible gender differences and similarities as well as developmental antecedents and consequences.

Joblessness and Discouragement

As urbanization increases at a rapid rate, chronic joblessness has become a major public policy issue in developing nations of the Third World and highly industrialized countries such as the United States. During the 1980s, the U.S. Department of Labor reported the most severe levels of joblessness since the Great Depression. Black youth consistently register the highest level of joblessness in the nation, a pattern that shows little evidence of reversing itself as we approach the twenty-first century. Black teenage unemployment was only 20 percent in 1968 but jumped to 50 percent by 1982. While official unemployment was well over 50 percent among black youth in many urban areas, it was only 20 percent for all teenagers and 10.8 percent for the general population. Therefore, when black youth seek gainful employment, as many as one of every two cannot find a job and still others become so discouraged that they discontinue actively searching for a job.

Discouragement in job search is particularly severe among black teenagers and young adults, but it continues to be a serious problem during the later adult years (Bowman, 1984; Ondeck, 1978; Wool, 1978). Official government statistics define jobless persons as "discouraged workers" when they do not actively search (behavioral component) for a job because of a belief (cognitive component) that there is no job for them. According to official statistics, blacks constitute about 10 percent of the population and 20 percent of the unemployed, but they make up as much as 40 percent of discouraged workers who stop looking for work because they believe their job search is hopeless. Going beyond official statistics, national studies of black Americans have found a degree of independence between the cognitive and behavioral components of job search discouragement (Bowman, 1984; Bowman, in press). While many black workers who believe that job search is hopeless stopped looking for work, many others who became hopeless continued to look actively for a job (Bowman, Jackson, Hatchett, and Gurin, 1982). These national studies show how official statistics fail to consider discouragement among the officially unemployed who become hopeless but continue their active job search; they also undercount the discouraged non-job-searchers who emphasize socially desirable reasons for not working.

The national studies of black Americans cited above also found that discouragement in job search was linked to both attributions of blame and psychological distress. Discouraged black youth and adults perceived that their chronic joblessness was caused primarily by labor market barriers (Bowman, 1984; Bowman, Jackson, Hatchett, and Gurin, 1982).

Rather than blaming only one factor, however, a more complex attributional pattern emerged where multiple factors were blamed for joblessness. In line with an attributional model of learned helplessness, discouraged respondents who blamed personal limitations (that is, lack of ability) rather than external labor market barriers as the major cause of their failure were less active in their job search (Bowman, Jackson, Hatchett, and Gurin, 1982). Going beyond the simplicity of helplessness models, however, jobless blacks also perceived blocked educational opportunities, racial inequities, lack of resources, and personal efforts as important obstacles in their search for good jobs (Bowman, 1984; Bowman, in press).

Rather than responding with a sense of helplessness, jobless black youth were even more likely than their older adult counterparts to remain active in their job search despite discouragement (Bowman, 1984; Bowman, Jackson, Hatchett, and Gurin, 1982). Regardless of job search behavior, the mere belief that the search was hopeless increased the risk of psychological distress—global life dissatisfaction, a sense of personal powerlessness, and low self-esteem. Yet among black youth who had lost hope during an earlier episode of unemployment, the link between discouragement and psychological distress failed to appear (Bowman, 1984). The latter finding suggests that emotional distress is linked to concurrent but not past discouragement in job search. Therefore, although discouragement in the search increased the risk for concurrent distress, its long-term psychosocial consequences may well depend on whether the job search eventually brings success.

Gender Differences

In this section, black male and female youth are compared on several indicators of objective and subjective aspects of job search strain. Official statistics show that black youth of both gender groups experience severely high levels of unemployment. However, black males may be at special risk of chronic joblessness and job search discouragement in the school-to-work transition. First, a growing gender gap in educational preparation has resulted in black males performing significantly worse than black females in elementary school, in secondary school, and in higher education (Hatchett, 1986; Riley, 1986; Trent, 1987). Second, the rapid displacement of unskilled industrial jobs has had more adverse effects on job loss and labor force dropout among black males than females (Allen and Farley, 1985; Bowman, 1988; Farley and Allen, 1987). Third, despite growing flexibility in gender roles, the "provider role" and "caretaker role" still appear to carry differential weights in the personal identities of men and women (Duvall, 1977; Troll, 1982). Although the economic stability of many black families has long depended on women finding employment, the emotional consequences of failure and success as a provider appear to be especially intense among black men (Bowman, 1985; Cazenave, 1981; Harrison, Bowman, and Beale, 1985; Liebow, 1967; Marsiglio, 1987). Moreover, due to present welfare policies, fewer black men than women qualify for public assistance during the transition from school to work.

Table 1 presents findings on gender differences in both chronic joblessness and discouragement among black youth during the adolescent-to-adult transition. These data were collected in a nationwide longitudinal survey of black youth in three-generation families. The 201 subjects were between the ages of nineteen and twenty-eight (youth transitional period) when reinterviewed for this study in 1983, after first being interviewed in 1979-1980 along with their parents and grandparents. This youth sample was systematically drawn from larger national probability samples by generating a national probability sample of 2,107 black adults eighteen years old or over; identifying the 53 percent subsample of this adult probability sample who were members of three-generation families; conducting an interview with other, randomly selected, family members of different generations to produce an intrafamilial cohort sample of grandparents, parents, and children at least fourteen years old; and then systematically selecting 116 females and 85 males to reinterview who were members of the youngest generation (children) in the three-generation sample. Because of the representativeness of the larger national probability sample, the youth subsample used in the current analysis of gender differences is national in scope and not restricted to any particular region, class, or sociodemographic group.

I found (Bowman, 1984) that 41 percent of the black youth in this sample were jobless, with 34 percent officially unemployed because they were actively searching for a job. As shown in Table 1, the youth vary widely in the duration of their unemployment, ranging from a few weeks to over a year (more than fifty-two weeks). What is striking about these data is not the gender differences but the similarity of males and females on this objective indicator of job search difficulty. Regardless of gender, the majority of black youth had been looking for work over two months and about a third over six months (at least twenty-seven weeks). Despite this gender similarity in duration of job search, females were less likely than males to actively search for a job (Bowman, 1984). While young black males were more often in the labor force, females more often reported that they were not searching for a job because of pregnancy, family demands, and school responsibilities.

When we turn to the subjective aspects of job search strain, Table 1 again reveals more gender similarity than difference on the two discouragement indicators. Almost one-half (47 percent) of the unemployed in both gender groups had come to believe that getting a job would be "ex-

Table 1. Gender Differences in Objective Job Search Difficulty and Discouragement Indicators

Indicator	Male (N)		Female (N)	
Duration of unemployment[a]				
1–3 weeks	19%		15%	
4–8 weeks	16		16	
9–16 weeks	19		22	
17–26 weeks	16		11	
27–52 weeks	23		20	
53 weeks or more	7		16	
	100%	(N = 31)	100%	(N = 37)
Current job search expectancy				
Impossible/extremely hard	47%		47%	
Fairly hard	34		47	
Not hard at all	19		6	
	100%	(N = 38)	100%	(N = 53)
Current job search hopelessness				
Lost hope	13%		21%	
Still hopeful	87		79	
	100%	(N = 39)	100%	(N = 57)

[a]Length of time looking for work.

tremely hard" to "almost impossible." Moreover, 21 percent of the females and 13 percent of the males had become so discouraged that they reported a complete loss of hope in their job search. Thus both objective and subjective aspects of job search strain were serious problems for the males and females as they strived to achieve full-fledged adulthood. To provide additional insight into job search strain in the school-to-work transition, youth were also asked a series of questions about past episodes of chronic joblessness, unemployment, and discouragement.

First each youth was asked: "Since leaving high school, how many different times have you been out of work for at least a six-month period, not counting your present unemployment?" In 1984, I reported that more than a third of the black youth had experienced at least one previous episode of unemployment that lasted six months or more in the school-to-work transition. To provide insight into job search strain among these black youth, Table 2 presents gender comparisons on past episodes of chronic joblessness, unemployment, and discouragement. Of the youth who had experienced a past period of chronic joblessness (no work for six months or more), one-half of the males (51 percent) and 45 percent of the females had already experienced two or more episodes. Among the unemployed who looked for work during these earlier episodes, about

Table 2. Gender Differences in Chronic Job Search Strains in School-to-Work Transition

Indicator	Male (N)		Female (N)	
Episodes of chronic joblessness (not working six months)				
One	49%		55%	
Two	32		24	
Three or more	19		21	
	100%	(N = 37)	100%	(N = 66)
Episodes of chronic unemployment (looking for work six months)				
One	67%		68%	
Two	22		24	
Three or more	11		8	
	100%	(N = 27)	100%	(N = 41)
Discouragement during first episodes of unemployment				
Lost hope	44%		42%	
Remained hopeful	56		58	
	100%	(N = 27)	100%	(N = 40)
Discouragement during subsequent episodes of unemployment				
Lost hope	31%		56%	
Remained hopeful	69		44	
	100%	(N = 13)	100%	(N = 16)

one in three within both gender groups had done so during two or more different periods. During the first unemployment episode, slightly more than 40 percent of both gender groups became so discouraged that they lost hope of finding a job. When youth experienced a subsequent period of chronic unemployment, however, a larger portion of the female (56 percent) than male (31 percent) respondents had lost hope.

In sum, the foregoing findings suggest that many black youth must cope with both objective and subjective aspects of chronic job search strain in the school-to-work transition. Not only were almost half of the black youth in the sample jobless, but one-third of the unemployed had actively sought work for more than six months, many had become so discouraged that they believed their job search was hopeless, and some had already experienced such extreme discouragement during more than one six-month episode of unemployment. These chronic job search difficulties appear to be experienced in similar proportions by both gender groups, despite the differential risks of black males for educational failure, postindustrial displacement, and labor force dropout. Perhaps, with fewer black men employed than in the past, increased provider-role pressures force more black women to seek jobs as a matter of personal and family economic survival (Bowman, 1988). Despite gender similarities in job search difficulties, the developmental implications of such difficulties may be quite different for black males and females (Bowman, 1989; Gary, 1981; Jones, 1989; Rodgers-Rose, 1980; Staples, 1982).

Developmental Issues

A life-span approach to chronic job search strain among black youth can provide a greater understanding of the developmental implications of this phenomenon. A life-span research framework not only has important theoretical relevance but can also inform public policy and preventive intervention. To be viable, a life-span approach to chronic job search strain during the adolescent-to-adult transitional stage should have at least two major features. First, it must be constructed upon a coherent *theoretical base* that clarifies both objective and subjective aspects of chronic job search strain. Second, it must include a *life cycle framework* that considers pivotal developmental antecedents and consequences of chronic job search strain in the school-to-work transition.

A Theoretical Model: Role Strain and Adaptation. An emerging literature on role-strain adaptation processes provides a coherent theoretical basis to conceptualize the operation of objective and subjective aspects of chronic job search strain (Allen and Vande Vliert, 1981; Baruch and Barnett, 1986; Barnett, Biener, and Baruch, 1987; Bowman, 1985, 1989; Pearlin, 1983; Sarbin and Allen, 1968). The *role strain* concept may be defined as objective difficulty, and subjective reactions to such difficulty, that impede the achievement of valued goals in a major life role (Bowman, 1989; Pearlin, Lieberman, Menaghan, and Mullan, 1981). As individuals engage in major life roles, *normative role strains* may be periodically produced by life transitions, stressful events, or other transient life problems (Felner, Faber, and Primavera, 1980; Goode, 1960). In contrast, *chronic role strains* may also occur when individuals face severe personal limitations, social-structural barriers, or conflicts at the person/environment interface (Kahn and others, 1964; Kessler, Price, and Wortman, 1985; Merton, 1968; Pearlin and Lieberman, 1979).

Role adaptation refers to the process through which individuals mobilize accessible resources, or fail to mobilize them, to cope with difficulty in a valued social role (Bowman, 1985; Cohen and Wills, 1985; Menaghan, 1983; Moos, 1976; Pearlin and others, 1981). Hence when barriers frustrate achievement strivings in a major life role, individuals may respond in either adaptive or maladaptive ways. While chronic role strains increase the risk of maladaptive responses, access to adaptive coping resources can mitigate emotional distress and promote instrumental behavior. In the role adaptation process, access to social and personal resources may empower individuals to perceive discouraging barriers as manageable rather than uncontrollable. Therefore, such resources may influence the manner in which chronic role barriers are perceived, interpreted, and evaluated to distinguish adaptive from maladaptive modes of coping (Pearlin and Schooler, 1978; Sarbin and Allen, 1968).

Building on expectancy-value theory, our ongoing program of research seeks to clarify social-psychological factors that differentiate adaptive from maladaptive coping among black youth and others at high risk of chronic strains in major life roles (Bowman, 1984, 1985, 1988, 1989, 1990a, 1990b; Bowman and Howard, 1985; Bowman and others, 1982). The specific role-strain adaptation model emerging from this research suggests, first, that maladaptive responses to objective difficulty in highly valued social roles tend to be exacerbated by *role discouragement* and *intrapunitive role attributions* and, second, that access to objective and subjective *cultural resources* facilitate adaptive over maladaptive modes of coping with chronic role strain. Guided by this basic role-strain adaptation model, we can conceptualize the nature, antecedents, and consequences of chronic job search strain among black youth.

Black youth, like other youth in society, are socialized to value success as students, workers, and family members (Boykin and Toms, 1985; Erikson, 1968; Jones, 1989; Merton, 1968). In a social-psychological sense, they come to think of themselves largely in terms of the social roles they aspire to play in life. Equally important, their self-evaluations depend heavily on work-role attainment and anticipated achievements in subsequent adult roles they esteem. As discussed earlier, despite the high stakes most black youth place on successful job search, they must often cope with pressing barriers, repeated failure, and discouragement (Adams and Mangum, 1978; Bowman, 1984; Malveaux, 1989). In the next section, a life-span approach to precursors and consequences of job search discouragement among black youth is considered.

A Life Cycle Framework. To identify pivotal antecedents and consequences of chronic job search strain in the school-to-work transition, we can extrapolate from a proliferating literature on life-span development (Baltes and Brim, 1980; Erikson, 1980; George, 1980; Levinson and others, 1978; Stevenson-Long, 1979; Van Hoose and Worth, 1982). According to life-span models, healthy human development requires one to progress through four critical stages of adulthood—preadult years, early adulthood, middle adulthood, and old age. During each period of this adult life cycle, mental health and successful aging depend on resolving conflicts and mastering tasks related to salient role strains. While Erikson and other adult development theorists provide a useful point of departure, a viable life-span approach to job search strain among black youth must have several unique features.

In contrast to other life-span paradigms, Figure 1 highlights specific role-strain processes necessary to conceptualize pivotal antecedents and consequences of job search strain among black youth in America (Bowman, 1989). In terms of antecedents, unresolved student-role strain (that is, history of educational failure, student-role discouragement) during the preadult years becomes a pivotal precursor of chronic job search strain (that is, long-term joblessness, job search discouragement) in the adolescent-to-adult transition (Bowman, in press; Sproat, Churchill, and Sheets, 1985; Williams, 1982; Wilson, 1978). In turn, chronic job search strain places black youth at risk for subsequent family- and elderly-role strains as they move through adulthood (Bowman, 1988; Liebow, 1967; Jackson and Gibson, 1985; Wilson, 1987). This succession of role strains has special developmental implications during the pre-, early, middle, and older adult years respectively. The focus on salient role performance goals, pressing role barriers, and critical role conflicts at each life cycle stage provides the basis for a unique developmental approach (Bowman, 1989).

Erikson and other life cycle theorists agree that salient role motivations usually shift as youth grow older and proceed from one stage of adulthood to the next. At each major transition point in the adult life cycle, salient goals systematically shift from educational preparation, to career consolidation, to familial fulfillment, and finally to dignified aging. Early failure among black youth in student roles often combines with impending work-role barriers to frustrate career, familial, and personal strivings that underpin adult development (Bowman, 1984, 1989; Boykin, 1983; Ogbu, 1974, 1988; Williams, 1982). Student- work- and family provider-role frustrations have special psychosocial relevance during successive life stages from the preadult years to old age. However, frustration of strivings in a given role may occur during more than one stage.

In addition to blocked educational opportunities, other discouraging structural barriers increase psychosocial risks among jobless black youth in the school-to-work transition. As suggested earlier, adverse effects of ineffective schools are made worse by the rapid displacement of unskilled industrial jobs, persistent racial antipathy, isolation in economically depressed inner cities, and a destructive, drug-based, neighborhood opportunity structure (Bowman, 1988, in press; Kinder, 1986; Jones, 1989; Wilson, 1987). Such job search barriers not only carry immediate risks for black youth but also combine with other pressing barriers in subsequent life roles to impede adult development. In psychosocial terms, successive barriers in student, work, family, and elderly roles can become major impediments to identity consolidation, intimate male–female bonding, family life satisfaction, and dignified aging.

Figure. 1 Antecedents and Consequences of Chronic Work-Role Strain in the Early Adulthood Transition

Stage	Salient Goals	Pressing Barriers	Critical Conflicts
Preadult years: student-role strain	Educational preparation	Ineffective public school	Student role discouragement vs. educational achievement
Early adulthood: work-role strain	Career consolidation	Postindustrial displacement	Job search discouragement vs. occupational attainment
Middle adulthood: provider-role strain	Familial fulfillment	Chronic employment problems	Provider role discouragement vs. husband/father success
Old age: elderly-role strain	Dignified aging	Inadequate retirement provisions	Elderly role discouragement vs. functional health

Source: Bowman, 1989, p. 127. © 1989 by R. L. Jones. Reprinted by permission.

Critical developmental tasks during successive adult stages involve successful coping with salient student-, work-, family- and elderly-role difficulties. However, repeated failure in each salient role may elicit discouragement, a sense of hopelessness, and psychosocial distress and eventually threaten cherished values. Such patterns of chronic role strain may involve a distressful and value-threatening approach/avoidance conflict: The tendency to approach valued goals in the salient life role may be countered by a tendency to avoid repeated failure. Motivation and commitment to valued roles may be severely tested by repeated role failures, aversive role discouragement, and emotional distress. If discouragement reaches the level of hopelessness, the pattern of distress in major life roles may be expressed in more severe psychosocial symptoms. Hence intense student-role conflicts may not only produce identity confusion in the school-to-work transition but may also increase the risk of isolation in male–female relations, stagnation as family providers, and despair in the elderly role.

While intense job search conflicts carry psychosocial risks among black youth, cultural resources that are transmitted across generations may facilitate adaptive over maladaptive modes of coping. We currently know far too little about the factors that differentiate black youth who capitulate to barriers in the school-to-work transition from those who somehow manage to beat the odds. I have suggested (Bowman, 1989) that adaptive cultural resources may combine with the successful resolution of student-role conflicts to facilitate adaptive coping with impending work-role barriers. A growing literature on black Americans supports the adaptive value of unique patterns of extended family networks and flexible family roles as well as subjective cultural resources such as strong kinship bonds, para-kin relations, ethnic coping orientations, and religion (Billingsley, 1968; Gurin and Epps, 1974; Hill, 1971; Morris, 1984; Jackson, McCullough, and Gurin, 1988; Neighbors, Jackson, Bowman, and Gurin, 1983). Like any other ethnic group, black Americans may transmit such cultural resources to each new generation to help them cope with the barriers they face in major life roles (Berry and Blassingame, 1982; Bowman and Howard, 1985; Harding, 1983; Martin and Martin, 1978). Rather than regarding them as mere reactions to oppression, Afrocentric scholars view these African American cultural patterns as essentially African forms that are strategically adapted to shifting economic, social, and ecological imperatives (Baldwin, 1981; DuBois, 1903; Herskovits, 1935; Nobles, 1988; Sudarkasa, 1988).

In psychosocial terms, adaptive cultural resources may empower black youth in two major ways (Bowman, 1989, 1990a; Bowman and Howard, 1985). First, cultural resources may nurture a general sense of personal efficacy by facilitating adaptive coping with student-role strain. Second, adaptive resources may enable youth to overcome impending barriers in the school-to-work transition. Social learning studies demonstrate processes through which role success at one developmental stage may increase a sense of personal empowerment and efficacy in coping with role barriers during subsequent stages (Bandura, 1986). Similarly, cultural resources that promote mastery of role barriers at one stage may provide the psychosocial basis for successful adaptation to future role strains. Personal empowerment, which is rooted in culture and prior student-role success, may be the basic formula for jobless black youth who beat the odds. Despite the virtues of indigenous resources, however, pressing structural barriers are likely to place black youth at alarming risk for chronic job search strain well into the twenty-first century. Therefore, future research must clarify both the theoretical and the practical implications of their prolonged transition from adolescence to adulthood.

Summary and Conclusion

Although many youth experience difficulty in the school-to-work transition, increasing numbers of black youth face more chronic difficulties that have far-reaching developmental implications. This chapter examines both objective and subjective aspects of chronic joblessness among black youth, with emphasis on gender differences in discouragement over job searches and related developmental issues. A life cycle approach to role strain and adaptation provides a coherent framework to guide theoretical inquiry into jobless black youth in America. Role-strain adaptation processes have special appeal because they provide a coherent conceptual base for studies on the nature, antecedents, and consequences of chronic difficulty in job search. Two basic notions in the proposed role-strain adaptation approach to joblessness among black youth are that discouragement in the job search and self-blame increase the risk of maladaptive responses to objective barriers and that objective and subjective cultural resources facilitate adaptive response patterns. The role-strain adaptation paradigm not only provides a parsimonious framework but also builds on a diverse theoretical and empirical literature (Barnett, Beiner, and Baruch, 1987; Bowman, 1989; Goode, 1960; Kahn and others, 1964; Merton, 1968; Pearlin, 1983; Sarbin and Allen, 1968). Role-strain adaptation models allow one to go beyond past studies on black youth, which have primarily been descriptive rather than theoretical and predictive.

In addition to the foregoing benefits, a major virtue of the life cycle approach to job search strain processes is its explanatory power throughout the life span (Allen and Vande Vliert, 1981; Erikson, 1980; George, 1980; Levinson and others, 1978). A life cycle framework avoids common misconceptions that occur with a narrow focus on job search strain among black youth that fails to consider the continuity in chronic role-strain adaptation processes. In a broader life-span framework, the interrelated concepts of human development and cultural adaptation have unique explanatory power. Elsewhere (Bowman, 1989) I have noted that

> to develop means to grow out of, to evolve from—where experiences at one life stage not only follow but emerge directly from preceding life experiences. The related concept of adaptation involves a continuing process of incorporating past experiences into new patterns to strategically meet the challenge of changing life demands without undue compromise [p. 142].

For black youth faced with chronic joblessness, effective adaptation may require preserving core cultural patterns from prior generations, while also transforming such core patterns into new strategies to cope with job search barriers in postindustrial America.

Chronic job search strain and related psychosocial problems among black youth do not just occur at a point in time; they evolve from interactions between past student-role experiences and adaptations to pressing labor market barriers. The youth transitional stage evolves from childhood and builds directly upon the adolescent experience, while at the same time forming the basis for experiences of middle adulthood and old age. Successful youth development may not only emerge from earlier student-role experiences but may also depend on the effective mobilization of cultural resources to cope with pressing job search barriers and related role conflicts. During this critical life cycle period, black youth must draw from accessible cultural resources to reinforce a sense of personal efficacy and overcome barriers in their path to employment. A maladaptive response to job search barriers may become a major impediment to future striving, but successful adaptation becomes a cornerstone for personal empowerment and reinforces a growing capacity to deal with subsequent role barriers.

The scientific value of a life cycle approach to job search strain and adaptation among black youth depends on its ability to stimulate theory-oriented research. Well-designed empirical studies on jobless black youth can help to build basic theory on role-strain processes and guide preventive intervention. To further develop a life cycle model of role strain and adaptation, future inquiry should consider the following questions. *As black youth proceed from adolescence to adulthood, what is the nature of their job search strain and how is it related to salient role strains during earlier and later life stages?* Survey research can describe dimensions of naturally occurring job search strains, and panel data may be particularly useful in charting relationships among successive student, job search, family, and elderly-role strains. *During the youth transitional period, how does chronic job search strain increase the risk of specific maladaptive response patterns?* Research on black youth should seek to unravel links between job search discouragement and specific patterns of psychosocial distress. *How do specific cultural resources facilitate adaptive coping with job search strain during the youth transitional stage?* Afrocentric studies on objective and subjective cultural resources may help to explain why some black youth are able to maintain a sense of hope, vitality, and persistence and even to excel against the odds. Ethnic kinship, para-kin patterns, coping orientations, and religious beliefs may reduce feelings of being overwhelmed, cut off, or dispirited in response to repeated rejection.

Despite common discontinuities between theory-driven research and practice, the utility of a theoretical approach must ultimately be tested through its application by practitioners. Research on the proposed life-span approach to chronic job search strain can inform policymakers, clinicians, and others working with black youth. In terms of primary prevention, the basic life-span approach to role-strain adaptation processes suggests that responsive educational policies are especially crucial. Educational policies that eliminate systematic barriers within ineffective public schools might prevent chronic student-role strain among black youth during the preadult years. In turn, greater success in the student role would reduce the risk of chronic job search difficulty in the school-to-work transition. "Effective schools" at the early childhood, elementary, and secondary levels must prepare more black youth for the postsecondary training they will need to attain jobs in a highly skilled labor market. Because of the structural barriers facing jobless black youth, however, policymakers should also provide *race-specific* affirmative action policies to ensure that racial discrimination does not restrict qualified black youth in the school-to-work transition and *non-race-specific* policies to reduce the adverse impact of postindustrial displacement on growing numbers of underprepared black youth who are isolated within depressed inner-city neighborhoods.

Psychologists, other human service professionals, and community leaders can also design interventions to reaffirm indigenous cultural resources, to promote proactive coping, and to mitigate destructive psychosocial effects of chronic job strain. As black youth move from one adult stage to the next, Afrocentric prevention strategies that reinforce adaptive cultural resources may be especially timely. Indigenous cultural strengths at the community, familial, and personal levels may enable more black youth to resolve job search conflicts in an adaptive manner. For example, the Urban League and other community organizations have begun to develop innovative culture-based interventions. These interventions are based on the premise that the risk of maladaptive responses to chronic job search strain increases when black youth are alienated from indigenous cultural resources—community support systems, extended kinship networks, and ethnic coping orientations. The systematic reaffirmation of such cultural strengths may empower individuals to reverse maladaptive response patterns in the role adaptation process. The mobilization of cultural resources may also help black youth devise more proactive strategies to overcome role barriers and avoid the potentially devastating impact of successive role strains.

In sum, the immediate prospects for black youth overcoming chronic job search strain may depend largely on culture-based personal empowerment. Despite the benefits of personal empowerment, however, long-term prevention of growing job search difficulty among black youth may depend even more on responsive educational and employment policies. Such public policy initiatives need to reduce the objective job search barriers that discourage so many black youth in the adolescent-to-adult transition. Without such responsive policies, successive role strains among jobless black youth may have far-reaching effects at the familial, community, and societal levels well into the twenty-first century.

References

Adams, A. V., and Mangum, G. L. *The Lingering Crisis of Youth Unemployment.* Kalamazoo, Mich.: W. E. Upjohn Institute, 1978.
Allen, V., and Vande Vliert, E. (eds.). *Role Transitions.* New York: Plenum, 1981.

Allen, W. R., and Farley, R. "The Shifting Social and Economic Tides of Black America, 1950-1980." *Annual Review of Sociology*, 1985, *12*, 277-306.
Anderson, B., and Sawhill, I. (eds.). *Youth Employment and Public Policy*. Englewood Cliffs, N.J.: Prentice-Hall, 1980.
Atwater, E. *Adolescence*. Englewood Cliffs, N.J.: Prentice-Hall, 1988.
Baldwin, J. "Notes on an Afrocentric Theory of Black Personality." *Western Journal of Black Studies*, 1981, *5*, 172-179.
Baltes, P. B., and Brim, O. G. (eds.). *Life Span Development and Behavior*. New York: Academic Press, 1980.
Bandura, A. *Social Foundations of Thought and Action: A Social-Cognitive Theory*. Englewood Cliffs, N.J.: Prentice-Hall, 1986.
Barnett, R. C., Beiner, L., and Baruch, G. K. *Gender and Stress*. New York: Free Press, 1987.
Baruch, G. K., and Barnett, R. C. "Consequences of Fathers' Participation in Family Work: Parents, Role Strain and Wellbeing." *Journal of Personality and Social Psychology*, 1986, *51*, 983-992.
Berry, M. F., and Blassingame, J. W. *Long Memory: The Black Experience in America*. New York: Oxford University Press, 1982.
Billingsley, A. *Black Families in White America*. Englewood Cliffs, N.J.: Prentice-Hall, 1968.
Bowman, P. J. "A Discouragement-Centered Approach to Studying Unemployment Among Black Youth: Hopelessness, Attributions and Psychological Distress." *International Journal of Mental Health*, 1984, *13*, 68-91.
Bowman, P. J. "Black Fathers and the Provider Role: Role Strain, Informal Coping Resource and Life Happiness." In A. W. Boykin (ed.), *Empirical Research in Black Psychology*. Washington, D.C.: National Institute of Mental Health, 1985.
Bowman, P. J. "Post-Industrial Displacement and Family Role Strains: Challenges to the Black Family." In P. Voydanof and L. C. Majka (eds.), *Families and Economic Distress*. Newbury Park, Calif.: Sage, 1988.
Bowman, P. J. "Research Perspectives on Black Men: Role Strain and Adaptation Across the Adult Life Cycle." In R. L. Jones (ed.), *Black Adult Development and Aging*. Berkeley: University of California Press, 1989.
Bowman, P. J. "Toward a Cognitive Adaptation Theory of Role Strain: Relevance of Research on Black Fathers." In R. Jones (ed.), *Advances in Black Psychology*. Berkeley, Calif.: Cobbs & Henry, 1990a.
Bowman, P. J. "Naturally Occurring Psychological Expectancies: Theory and Measurement in Black Populations." In R. L. Jones (ed.), *Handbook of Tests and Measurements for Black Populations*. Berkeley, Calif.: Cobbs & Henry, 1990b.
Bowman, P. J. "Joblessness: Beyond Official Statistics." In J. S. Jackson, P. J. Bowman, G. Gurin, S. J. Hatchett, and M. B. Tucker (eds.), *Black American Life: Findings from a National Survey*. Newbury Park, Calif.: Sage, in press.
Bowman, P. J., and Howard, D. S. "Race-Related Socialization, Motivation and Academic Achievement: A Study of Black Youth in Three-Generation Families." *Journal of the Academy of Child Psychiatry*, 1985, *24*, 134-141.
Bowman, P. J., Jackson, J. S., Hatchett, S. J., and Gurin, G. "Joblessness and Discouragement Among Black Americans." *Economic Outlook U.S.A.*, 1982, Autumn, 85-88.
Boykin, A. W. "The Academic Performance of Afro-American Children." In J. Spence (ed.), *Achievement and Achievement Motives*. San Francisco: Freeman, 1983.
Boykin, A. W., and Toms, F. D. "Black Child Socialization: A Conceptual Frame-

work." In H. P. McAdoo and J. C. McAdoo (eds.), *Black Children.* Newbury Park, Calif.: Sage, 1985.

Cazenave, N. A. "Black Men in America: The Quest for 'Manhood.' " In H. P. McAdoo (ed.), *Black Families.* Newbury Park, Calif.: Sage, 1981.

Cohen, S., and Wills, T. A. "Stress, Social Support, and the Buffering Hypothesis." *Journal of Personality and Social Psychology,* 1985, *48,* 393-407.

DuBois, W.E.B. *The Negro American Family.* Cambridge, Mass.: MIT Press, 1903.

Duvall, E. *Marriage and Family Development.* (5th ed.) New York: Lippincott, 1977.

Erikson, E. H. *Identity, Youth and Crisis.* New York: Norton, 1968.

Erikson, E. H. *Identity and the Life Cycle.* New York: Norton, 1980.

Farley, R., and Allen, W. R. *The Color Line and the Quality of American Life.* New York: Russell Sage, 1987.

Felner, R. D., Faber, S. S., and Primavera, J. "Transitions and Stressful Life Events: A Model of Primary Prevention." In R. H. Price, R. F. Ketterer, B. C. Bader, and J. Monahan (eds.), *Prevention and Mental Health: Research, Policy and Practice.* Newbury Park, Calif.: Sage, 1980.

Freeman, R. B., and Wise, D. A. *The Youth Employment Problem: Its Nature, Causes and Consequences.* Chicago: University of Chicago Press, 1982.

Gary, L. E. (ed.). *Black Men.* Newbury Park, Calif.: Sage, 1981.

George, L. K. *Role Transitions in Later Life.* Belmont, Calif.: Brooks/Cole, 1980.

Goode, W. J. "A Theory of Role Strain." *American Sociological Review,* 1960, *11,* 483-496.

Gurin, P., and Epps, E. *Black Consciousness, Identity and Achievement.* New York: Wiley, 1974.

Harding, V. *There Is a River: The Struggle for Freedom in America.* New York: Vintage Books, 1983.

Harrison, A. O., Bowman, P. J., and Beale, R. L. "Role Strain, Coping Resources, and Psychological Well-Being Among Black Working Mothers." In A. W. Boykin (ed.), *Empirical Research in Black Psychology.* Washington, D.C.: National Institute of Mental Health, 1985.

Hatchett, D. "A Conflict of Reasons and Remedies." *Crisis,* 1986, *93,* 36-46.

Herskovits, M. J. "Social History of the Negro." In C. Murchinson (ed.), *A Handbook of Social Psychology.* London: Oxford University Press, 1935.

Hill, R. *Strengths of Black Families.* New York: Emerson Hall, 1971.

Jackson, J. S., and Gibson, R. "Work and Retirement Among Black Elderly." In Z. Blau (ed.), *Work, Leisure, and Retirement Among Black Elderly.* Greenwich, Conn.: JAI Press, 1985.

Jackson, J. S., McCullough, W., and Gurin, G. "Socialization Environment and Identity Development in Black Families." In H. McAdoo (ed.), *Black Families.* Newbury Park, Calif.: Sage, 1988.

Jones, R. L. *Black Adolescence.* Berkeley, Calif.: Cobbs & Henry, 1989.

Kahn, R. L., Wolfe, D. M., Quinn, R. P., Snoek, J. D., and Rosenthal, R. A. *Organizational Stress: Studies in Interrole Conflict and Ambiguity.* New York: Wiley, 1964.

Keniston, D. "Youth: A 'New' Stage of Life." *American Scholar,* 1970, *39,* 631-654.

Kessler, R. C., Price, R. H., and Wortman, C. B. "Social Factors in Psychopathology: Stress, Social Support and Coping Processes." *Annual Review of Psychology,* 1985, *31,* 531-572.

Kinder, D. R. "The Continuing American Dilemma: White Resistance to Racial Change 40 Years After Myrdal." *Journal of Social Issues,* 1986, *42,* 151-171.

Levinson, D. F., Darrow, C. N., Klein, E. B., Levinson, M. H., and McKee, B. *The Seasons of a Man's Life.* New York: Ballantine, 1978.

Liebow, E. *Tally's Corner: A Study of Street Corner Men.* Boston: Little, Brown, 1967.

Malveaux, J. "Transitions: The Black Adolescent and the Labor Market." In R. D. Jones (ed.), *Black Adolescence.* Berkeley, Calif.: Cobbs & Henry, 1989.

Marsiglio, W. "Commitment to Social Fatherhood: Predicting Adolescent Males' Intentions to Live with Their Child and Partner." *Journal of Marriage and the Family,* 1987.

Martin, E. P., and Martin, J. M. *The Black Extended Family.* Chicago: University of Chicago Press, 1978.

Menaghan, E. G. "Individual Coping Efforts: Moderators of the Relationship Between Life Stress and Mental Health Outcomes." In H. B. Kaplan (ed.), *Psychosocial Stress: Trends in Theory and Research.* New York: Academic Press, 1983.

Merton, R. K. *Social Theory and Social Structure.* New York: Free Press, 1968.

Moos, R. H. *Human Adaptation: Coping with Life Stress.* Lexington, Mass.: Heath, 1976.

Morris, A. *Origins of the Civil Rights Movement: Black Communities Organizing for Change.* New York: Free Press, 1984.

Neighbors, H. W., Jackson, J. S., Bowman, P. J., and Gurin, G. "Stress, Coping and Black Mental Health." *Journal of Prevention in Human Service,* 1983, *2,* 5-29.

Nobles, W. "African-American Family Life: An Instrument of Culture." In H. P. McAdoo (ed.), *Black Families.* Newbury Park, Calif.: Sage, 1988.

Ogbu, J. *The Next Generation.* New York: Academic Press, 1974.

Ogbu, J. "Black Education: A Cultural-Ecological Perspective." In H. P. McAdoo (ed.), *Black Families.* Newbury Park, Calif.: Sage, 1988.

Ondeck, C. "Discouraged Workers' Link to Jobless Rate Reaffirmed." *Monthly Labor Review,* Oct. 1978, pp. 40-42.

Pearlin, L. I. "Role Strains and Personal Stress." In H. B. Kaplan (ed.), *Psychosocial Stress: Trends in Theory and Research.* New York: Academic Press, 1983.

Pearlin, L. I., and Lieberman, M. A. "Social Sources of Emotional Distress." In R. Simmons (ed.), *Research in Community and Mental Health.* Greenwich, Conn.: JAI Press, 1979.

Pearlin, L. I., and Schooler, C. "The Structure of Coping." *Journal of Health and Social Behavior,* 1978, *19,* 1-21.

Pearlin, L. I., Lieberman, M. A., Menaghan, E. G., and Mullan, S. "The Stress Process." *Journal of Health and Social Behavior,* 1981, *22,* 337-356.

Riley, N. "Footnotes of a Culture at Risk." *Crisis,* 1986, *93,* 23-45.

Rodgers-Rose, L. F. (ed.). *The Black Woman.* Newbury Park, Calif.: Sage, 1980.

Sarbin, T. R., and Allen, V. L. "Role Theory." In G. Lindzey and E. Aronson (eds.), *Handbook of Social Psychology.* Reading, Mass.: Addison-Wesley, 1968.

Sproat, K. V., Churchill, H., and Sheets, C. *The National Longitudinal Surveys of Labor Market Experience: An Annotated Bibliography of Research.* Lexington, Mass.: Lexington Books, 1985.

Staples, R. *Black Masculinity: The Black Man's Role in American Society.* San Francisco: Black Scholar Press, 1982.

Stevenson-Long, J. *Adult Life: Developmental Processes.* Palo Alto, Calif.: Mayfield, 1979.

Sudarkasa, N. "Interpreting the African Heritage in Afro-American Family Organization." In H. P. McAdoo (ed.), *Black Families.* Newbury Park, Calif.: Sage, 1988.

Trent, W. T. "Characteristics and Patterns of Black Two-Year Enrollment and Degree Attainment." In B. T. Ridgeway and C. E. Morris (eds.), *Strategies for Improving the Status of Blacks in Secondary Education.* Normal: Illinois State University/ICBCHE, 1987.

Troll, L. W. *Continuation: Adult Development and Aging.* Belmont, Calif.: Brooks/Cole, 1982.

Van Hoose, W. H., and Worth, M. R. *Adulthood in the Life Cycle.* Dubuque, Iowa: Brown, 1982.

Williams, J. (ed.). *The State of Black America.* New York: National Urban League, 1982.

Wilson, W. J. *The Declining Significance of Race: Blacks and Changing American Institutions.* Chicago: University of Chicago Press, 1978.

Wilson, W. J. *The Truly Disadvantaged: The Inner City, the Underclass, and Public Policy.* Chicago: University of Chicago Press, 1987.

Wool, H. *Discouraged Workers, Potential Workers, and National Employment Policy.* Washington, D.C.: National Commission for Manpower Policy, 1978.

Phillip J. Bowman is assistant professor of psychology and Afro-American studies at the University of Illinois, Champaign. At the time of this writing, he was a visiting senior research fellow with the University of Michigan's Institute for Social Research.

With increasing age, children explain wealth and poverty by referring to individual differences in work, effort, and intelligence rather than social-structural or political factors. Such explanations of inequality support a belief in a just world where the "losers" are viewed as obtaining their just due.

The Development of Concepts of Economic and Social Inequality

Robert L. Leahy

Although social class and other categories of stratification (such as race, gender, age, and intelligence) have often been used as independent variables in the classification of subjects, relatively little research had been done until recently on how children and adolescents come to view stratification. Certainly Clark and Clark's (1947) landmark work on racial differences in the perception of dolls was a noted exception to this tendency to view stratification as an independent variable in psychological research.

The study of how children come to understand, explain, justify, and challenge stratification may be viewed as a central, and necessary, component of our understanding of the socialization process. One might argue that the essential purpose of socialization is precisely this in a society—that is, to assure allegiance and consensus in the perception of stratification (Merton, 1957; Parsons, 1960). Failure to provide consensus and allegiance results in disruptive and competing interests among different groups.

Over the last decade I have been interested in how children and adolescents construct a variety of social stratification systems. My colleagues and I have studied the development of concepts of economic inequality (Leahy, 1981, 1983a, 1983b), sex roles (Leahy and Shirk, 1984), intelligence (Leahy and Hunt, 1983), and age maturity (Leahy and Bresler, 1982). In these investigations we were generally guided by a cognitive-developmental model to the study of social cognition. Here I summarize our findings on the development of concepts of economic inequality and suggest some cognitive-developmental trends in the construction of other aspects of social inequality. Further, I propose that there are "costs" of social-cognitive development resulting in increasing tendencies to blame those (including the self) who fall below the average in different status hierarchies (Leahy, 1983c, 1985).

Theoretical Models of Stratification

The study of the development of concepts of social inequality must begin with an epistemology of what these concepts might be in their final, developed form—specifically, what is the individual developing into?—and how we would characterize the child's knowledge in relation to the adult's knowledge of inequality. There are three models of relevance here—conflict, functional, and cognitive-developmental.

The conflict model emphasizes the view that perception of the stratification system will depend on the different strata occupied by individuals (Marx, 1966; Weber, 1946). For example, merchants and blue-collar industrial workers would view work, the products of labor, and class relations in a considerably different manner from one another. Those experiencing displacement, conflict, or exploitation within the stratification system would be most likely to achieve an understanding of class interests and historical factors, according to this model. This model of stratification concepts describes a rather pessimistic view of the endpoint of development and sheds little light on the developmental process. In regard to the study of the development of these concepts, however, we should expect from this model that different groups (classes, races, genders) would have disparate and conflicting views of the stratification process and that increasing age, marked by supposed increased understanding of "class consciousness," should result in increased challenge to the stratification system.

In contrast to the conflict model, the functional model of socialization proposes that stratification concepts are widely shared and serve to justify and stabilize the stratification system (Merton, 1957; Parsons, 1960). An implication of functionalism is that socialization is viewed as the increasing allegiance to the stratification hierarchy. Thus one might expect from this model that consensus, justification, and views of stabilized stratification should be reflected in the stratification concepts of children and that these qualities should be more widely established with increasing age.

The cognitive-developmental model I propose (termed structural-developmental) draws on the work of Piaget (1970) and Kohlberg (1969). Specifically, I propose that stratification concepts undergo (1) qualitative change with age reflecting (2) a natural ordering of concepts that reflect (3) cognitive level. Further, these stratification concepts are marked by consistency across different themes—that is, concepts of intelligence, economic class, sex differences, deviance, and personality share similar structural properties. I refer to this as *organizational unity*. Finally, cognitive or stage transitions are viewed as a consequence of cognitive disequilibrium such that individuals experiencing greater conflict will more rapidly attain higher levels in that domain of conflict. This proposition suggests that greater class consciousness (which is a higher level of conceptualizing economic stratification) should be manifested by more economically deprived individuals. This latter proposal is consistent with the conflict theory described above. Unlike conflict theory, however, cognitive-developmental theory offers no clear prediction regarding increasing justification, challenge, or stabilization with increased age. We shall now examine several implications of the cognitive-developmental approach in more detail.

Natural Ordering of Concepts. In contrast to a strict associationist or social learning theory model of social-cognitive development, the structural-developmental model proposes that there is a natural ordering of social concepts such that simple concepts are necessary but not sufficient precursors of higher-order concepts. Three general levels of stratification concepts are specified—peripheral, psychological, and systemic. Causal concepts of each of these phenomena are also ordered sequentially.

Peripheral concepts of persons refer to the external, observable, tangible qualities of individuals, such as their clothing, physical attributes, and simple behavior. Psychological concepts of persons refer to inferred, internal states of individuals, such as motivations, thoughts, feelings, and dispositions. Evidence of the sequentiality of these descriptions is found in studies of how children describe others and themselves, showing that increased age is associated with decreased reference to peripheral and increased reference to "central" (here, "psychological") concepts of persons (Livesley and Bromley, 1973). Similarly, in studies of concepts of deviance (Coie and Pennington, 1976; Paget, 1983), intelligence (Leahy and Hunt, 1983), and sex roles (Williams, Bennett, and Best, 1975) peripheral or behavioral dimensions are the first dimensions identified by younger children, with psychological dimensions becoming increasingly more important with increasing age.

These studies, as well as the results of the class-concepts study to be described in more detail below, point to developmental regularities regarding peripheral and psychological concepts suggesting organizational unity. Why are psychological concepts more "highly developed" concepts? First, peripheral concepts are simply descriptions of behavior, whereas psychological concepts are generalizations about behavior—that is, they are classifications of behavior. Second, psychological concepts are inferences about unobservables and, therefore, are more abstract than peripheral concepts. Finally, psychological concepts are attempts to "explain" behavior by reference to thoughts or dispositions, whereas behavioral descriptions may simply be seen as descriptions without explanations. In other words, at the psychological concept level the individual is attempting to answer *why* someone did something.

A further step in the hierarchy of concepts of stratification is *systemic thinking*. By systemic thinking I mean the ability to recognize that the individual belongs to social groups that may affect the way he thinks and behaves and that the individual's behavior affects other people who then respond to his behavior—that is, systemic thinking is interactive. Probably very few adults think systemically with any regularity. Evidence related to the development of systemic thinking has been presented by Selman (1980) in his studies of role-taking development. Selman found that preadolescents had considerable difficulty taking the third-person perspective on interaction—that is, the ability to see the self and others in mutual interaction from the perspective of another observer. This may be a rudimentary level of systemic thinking that involves at higher levels the ability to recognize how one produces behavior in others and how others produce behavior in oneself, thereby maintaining the stability of social interaction systems (Leahy, in press). For example, the ability to understand Patterson's "coercion cycle" is an example of the ability to engage in this higher level of systemic thinking.

Applied specifically to the development of stratification concepts, systemic thinking entails what I have called *sociocentric thinking*. This involves the ability to understand that an individual's membership in a group (such as an economic class) has implications for life-quality opportunities (legal rights, employment, education, health)—which I refer to as *life chances* (see Weber, 1946). Also, sociocentric conceptions refer to awareness that class membership affects how people view the stratification system or how they are viewed by others occupying different classes. I refer to this as *class consciousness* (Marx, 1966).

Cognitive-Development and Stratification Concepts. The structural-developmental model proposes that nonsocial and social-cognitive development are marked by *structural isomorphism*. This does not imply that one domain (for example, the nonsocial) is attained prior to the other as Kohlberg (1969) has argued. Rather, the structural model proposed here suggests that social and nonsocial cognition show similar sequences in development such that development in one domain affects development in another domain. Thus we would expect positive correlations of performances on structurally similar social and nonsocial stimuli as well as positive correlations within a single domain. We may refer to this as the *organizational unity principle*.

According to the cognitive-developmental model, decentration is an ability that is attained primarily through social interaction rather than through the manipulation or experimentation with the nonsocial world (Feffer, 1970). Decentration refers to the ability to coordinate different perspectives within a system—for example, to be able to reconstruct the perspectives of different people in a spatial plane. Social interaction, which provides the opportunity for exposure to conflicting opinions and the opportunity to construct rules with peers, facilitates decentration. In fact, this emphasis on social interaction as a source of development of cognition was Piaget's earlier position (1926, 1965), which gave way to more formal structuralist descriptions of operative intelligence in his later writings (for example, Piaget, 1970). For the present discussion, I see decentration as a result of both social and nonsocial factors. Unlike Piaget, however, I view decentration as a life-span process of development such that there is an ongoing process (or possibility) of decentering from one's own thought to view that thought within a system. This system may be dyadic (for example, a couple interacting), familial, role-specified (for example, sex roles), class-stratified, or racial. We should be mindful that Piaget, who first advanced the idea of decentration, emphasized the coordination of elements within a system. Although his original discussion focused on spatial reasoning, the principle is applicable to all systems as Piaget (1970) emphasized in his volume on structuralism.

At the concrete operational level (by the age of eight), decentration is reflected in the ability to refocus on two dimensions and to coordinate these dimensions—for example, the ability to recognize that a decrease in height may be compensated by a decrease in width to conserve volume (Feffer, 1970). Younger, preoperational children tend to be centered on the physical stimuli and cannot anticipate correctly their possible transformations. This ability underlies role taking, not only in coordinating perspectives but also in being able to infer the psychological qualities of persons such as thoughts and dispositions. Further, decentration is involved in the ability to find causes of psychological processes—such as deviance—with increased decentering implied by recognizing that ultimate causes may be more important than immediate causes in explaining another's behavior (Coie and Pennington, 1976; Paget, 1983). More advanced decentration is essential in the ability to understand individuals within social systems—specifically, sociocentric thinking or class consciousness. As Elkind (1967) has indicated, the ability to decenter—to stand outside the self and view the self from another's perspective—continues beyond concrete operations into the formal operational period.

One may view any stratification system as a set of rules that maintain conventions of distributive justice—that is, rules that guide and justify unequal treatment of individuals within a group or society. "Postconventional" thinking involves the ability to stand apart from these conventions and question either their utility or justice. This is the difference between Kohlberg's (1969) conventional and postconventional levels of moral judgment, but postconventional thinking may be more general than moral judgments and may be viewed as any thinking that challenges a set of rules (see Turiel, 1978). The sequential model of cognitive development suggests that three stages should be discernible: (1) the absence of knowledge of conventions; (2) knowledge of conventions accompanied by the belief that these conventions are immutable; and (3) recognition that conventions may change.

In our study of stratification concepts, we have found some evidence of these three stages. In conceptions of sex roles, younger children (four years old) lack knowledge of sex-stereotyped behavior, followed by rigid classification at age six, and ending at age eight with the recognition that "sex-typed" behavior may be manifested by either gender (Leahy and Shirk, 1984). Similarly, in our study of class concepts there was increasing justification of inequality with increasing age, but this tendency decreased for some adolescents who challenged inequality (Leahy, 1983b).

A second cognitive attainment with reference to stratification concepts is classificatory skill. Very young children (age four) engage in configurative sorting such that they arrange objects into a design rather than distinct classes. This is followed by exhaustive sorting—the classification of objects by a single dimension that all class members share (such as color). Later, this gives way to multiple classification such that classes, once formed, can be resorted into other categories. Once a class of red objects is formed, for example, they may be resorted into other classes of triangles and circles (Inhelder and Piaget, 1958). As mentioned above, we have found (Leahy and Shirk, 1984) that sex-role stereotypes developed in the expected age sequence and that the ability to classify social and nonsocial stimuli was positively correlated. This supported the organizational unity principle.

Finally, conceptions of distributive justice develop with age. Piaget (1965) proposed that between the ages of six and eleven there is a change from authority-based to equality-based to equity-based conceptions of justice. For example, the younger child (age six) gives precedence to the authority of elders; this unilateral respect results in the view that what elders have decided must be right. At about seven or eight the child shifts to a belief in the equal distribution of rewards without considering individual differences in performance or needs. In contrast, older children (age eleven) use an equity principle allocating greater reward based on merit. Several studies have yielded mixed findings as to whether equity gains precedence over equality in reward allocation as the child develops (Hook, 1982, 1983; Lane and Coon, 1972; Lerner, 1974; Leventhal and Lane, 1970). As a formalistic or structural model, equity is a more complex distributive model since it involves comparisons of relative inputs of different performers, while equality is a simple equal distribution. In our study of class concepts we examined whether equity concepts gain precedence over equality distributions.

Overview of Class-Concepts Study

There were 720 subjects drawn from four age groups (six, eleven, fourteen, and seventeen), black and white, from four social classes (lower to upper middle), in three cities (New York, Boston, and Washington, D.C.). All subjects, except sixty-seven white adolescents who responded to questions in written format, were individually interviewed between 1976 and 1978. Subjects from predominantly black schools were interviewed by two black graduate students while the other subjects were interviewed by white graduate students. Each subject was asked the following questions:

1. Describe rich people. What are they like?
2. Describe poor people. What are they like?
3. How are rich people different from poor people?
4. How are rich people the same as poor people? What do they have in common?
5-6. Why are some people rich (poor) while others are poor (rich)?
7-8. Should some people be rich (poor) while others are poor (rich)?
9. How could a poor person get rich some day?
10. What would have to happen so that there would be no poor people?
11. How could you get rich some day?

Answers to these questions were tape-recorded and scored into content categories developed on the basis of the person perception and moral development literature and on sociological models of economic stratification. Categories were mutually exclusive, resulting in scorable responses for most subjects. Interjudge reliability was satisfactory (see Leahy, 1981 and 1983a, for more details).

Descriptions of Rich and Poor People. In order to focus our attention on the pattern of age trends, I have provided a summary of levels of social class concepts derived from the data of this study (see Exhibit 1). This table shows that many of the expected developmental trends were supported. However, we shall examine in more detail the individual trends as well as the interesting class and race qualifications to the developmental sequence.

There were substantial decreases with age in references to the peripheral characteristics of rich and poor people and comparisons of how they were different from each other. There was increasing emphasis on the psychological qualities of people, such as their thoughts and traits. Thus younger children described classes in terms of their possessions (or lack of possessions) and by reference to appearance or behavior. Older children and adolescents were more likely to refer to thoughts, abilities, and personality ("smart," "lazy," "don't want to work"). Older lower-class sub-

Exhibit 1. Conceptions of Class

Level I: Peripheral-Dependent Conceptions (Ages 6–11)
Here the focus in descriptions is on the observable, external qualities of class, such as possessions and appearances. Explanations of class differences lack causal reasoning and focus on the definitional or peripheral aspects of wealth and poverty. Although there is concern for consequences to the poor, class differences may be justified because the rich and poor meet the definitional criteria of class. Mobility and social change are viewed largely in terms of either the rich or others helping people by giving them money. The child views the economy as functioning out of benevolence for the poor or for the child's own interests.

Level II: Psychological Conceptions (Ages 11–14)
At this level, classes are described in terms of their inferred psychological qualities, such as traits, thoughts, and motivations. Classes are seen as being similar primarily because they share peripheral commonalities (for example, "Both are people"). Inequality is explained in terms of differences in work, education, effort, and intelligence. Class differences are challenged by equality principles or justified by equity considerations. Mobility is seen largely in terms of education, effort, work, and investment. Social change is viewed in terms of either the rich sharing their wealth or the poor gaining education, working hard, and getting jobs. The economy is seen as rewarding merit reflected by individual differences in inputs.

Level III: Sociocentric Conceptions (Ages 14–17)
Here the descriptions focus on differences in life chances and class consciousness. Classes are viewed as similar because they share psychological commonalities. Explanations still focus on equity. There is an increasing emphasis on the difficulty of changing the social system and claims that social change would meet with resistance by the rich. Changing the social structure is viewed as one way to change poverty. The economy is seen as being functionally based on equity principles, although there is a recognition of competing class interests. The economy is viewed in impersonal terms such that its functioning is seen as a reflection of the invisible hand of earned merit or as the expression of the interests of the wealthy. Emphasis is on conflict (for example, class consciousness) or the futility of conflict (for example, fatalism).

jects were more likely than others to refer to the thoughts of the poor—a finding consistent with conflict theory. In contrast, upper-middle-class subjects more often described poor people in terms of traits. This finding is consistent with the view that poor children are better at taking the perspective of the poor, thus seeing the world from the "thoughts of the poor." This is similar to the actor–observer bias in person perception, such that observers are more likely to attribute personality traits to others than they are to themselves.

There was an increase in adolescence in describing the class consciousness of the rich—consistent with cognitive-developmental theory. Inconsistent with conflict theory, however, these descriptions were more common in describing rich than poor people and there were no class or race differences in descriptions of class consciousness.

Younger children often found no basis of similarity between the rich and poor; ten-year-olds claimed that they were both people or had similar behavior; adolescents were more likely than others to claim they had similar thoughts. Apparently, the first criterion of similarity is peripheral qualities, while during adolescence psychological and sociocentric qualities (for example, both are citizens) become more salient. The findings for these analyses were predominantly age effects with few interactions or main effects associated with race or class.

These findings are consistent with other data on concepts of intelligence. In a study by Leahy and Hunt (1983), younger children had difficulty finding any basis of similarity between intelligent and unintelligent people. Similarly, in our study of sex-role stereotyping (Leahy and Shirk, 1984) we found that young children (age six) had difficulty anticipating that males and females could both engage in opposite-sex-typed behavior.

The class-concepts data, as well as data on other aspects of stratification concepts, suggest four levels of stereotyping: (1) failure to engage in stereotyping; (2) rigid classification with denial of similarities; (3) stereotyping but recognition of peripheral similarities; and (4) stereotyping but recognition of psychological and systemic (sociocentric) similarities. One conclusion that summarizes this pattern of results is that once stereotypes are formed they become less stereotypic with increased age.

Explanations of Economic Inequality. Clear cognitive-developmental age trends in explanations of economic inequality emerged in our study. Younger children explained wealth and poverty primarily in terms of differences in possessions, inheritance, or the use of money—all peripheral descriptions. Psychological causes of inequality gained salience at ages eleven and fourteen—emphasizing work, effort, education, and intelligence. Thus increasing age was associated with explaining inequality by claiming that the rich and poor are different kinds of people, a finding consistent with their descriptions and comparisons. Examples of explanations by younger children are that poor people "can't buy a job," "they have no money," "they got no food," or "they spend their money on dumb things." Older children and adolescents explained inequality by claiming that "rich people have better education," "they're smarter," "they have better jobs," or "they work harder."

Contrary to conflict theory, there were very few references to sociocentric conceptions even during adolescence. There were generally similar age trends for both blacks and whites; inequality became increasingly legitimated by reference to individual differences rather than social-structural or political factors. In fact, contrary to conflict theory, it was the seventeen-year-old lower-class males who were most likely to view wealth in terms of intelligence. These data are in clear support of the functionalist model of socialization.

Consistent with the concrete focus of young children, the six-year-olds justified inequality by reference to the definitional differences between the classes—that is, rich people should be rich because they have money. Equality challenges to poverty (but not wealth) increased at age fourteen but decreased at seventeen. The idea that the rich should help the poor increased at age eleven but decreased after. This curvilinear age trend for equality norms was due to two developments in justifying inequality during adolescence: First, there was an increase in behavior-contingent justifications ("If you work hard, you should be rich"); second, there was an increase in fatalistic justifications ("There's always going to be poor people—that's human nature").

Two reasons are postulated to account for this curvilinear age trend for equality and equity concepts. The first cause—social-cognitive development—refers to the fact that older children and adolescents have greater capacity to identify individual psychological differences and greater ability to engage in social comparison and seriation of individual talent. These individual differences then become the basis for equity judgments. A second cause—functionalist socialization—refers to the shift from the mutuality and equality of the child's peer group to the meritocracy of the school culture that places greater emphasis on stratification in later school grades.

There was minor support for the conflict model: Whites were more likely than blacks to use fatalistic justifications, and lower-class subjects were more likely to show concern for the poor. However, the functionalist model received greater support than the conflict model. There was increasing justification of inequality with increasing age—for all classes and for both blacks and whites. In fact, the belief that inequality is fated would appear to conflict with a Piagetian view that formal operations during adolescence facilitate counterfactual thinking. One might argue that the functionalist socialization to perceive inequality as legitimate is so strong as to override formal operational thinking. Conflict theory emphasizes sociocentrism (class concepts, life chances, class conflict, class resistance to economic change); see Marx (1966) and Weber (1946). There were almost no challenges (less than 6 percent) of inequality referring to sociocentric factors. Class consciousness is not a major factor in the thinking of American youth.

Social Change and Individual Mobility

The data on concepts of social change offer strong support to a functionalist model. One response of special relevance to functionalist theory—because it appears to be the hallmark of the functionalist view that societal complexity necessitates stratification (Parsons, 1960)—is the view held by many adolescents that economic inequality is a necessary or fated quality of society. The fatalism of inequality is not based on a view that classes would actively *resist* change; rather, it reflects a view that human nature and complex society *require* stratification. Further, socialization to the "legitimacy" of inequality is reflected in the fact that equity concepts of change (that is, "poor people could work harder") increased substantially by age eleven. The view that inequality could be ended by others (that is, the rich) giving to the poor increased between ages six and eleven and decreased substantially thereafter. Thus legitimization of economic inequality took the form of fatalistic and equity concepts and the decrease of equalization concepts during adolescence.

There was also support for conflict theory regarding social change concepts. Blacks were more likely than whites to emphasize changing the social structure, and upper-middle-class subjects were more likely than others to claim that changing values could end poverty. The present data do not provide a basis for determining the children's views concerning whose or what values should change and what new values could be attained. However, the impression one gains from the interviews is that individual attitudes toward work (that is, equity values) are the most commonly mentioned or implied values. Middle-class whites were more likely than other groups to deny the possibility of change. Resistance to change was found with frequency only among lower-class adolescents, especially males.

Cognitive-developmental theory gains support in that sociocentric concepts increased during adolescence. This age trend was demonstrated for all classes and both races but was qualified by the interaction effects mentioned above.

Concepts of individual change showed strong developmental trends. Young children personified their own mobility by claiming that they or a poor person could become rich by asking others for money. ("You can go to the bank and ask them for money" or "The waiter could give me money.") Equity conceptions increased with age—for example, references to education or effort. Again, for all classes and both races there were similar age trends for most of these analyses. There were only two notable exceptions to this pattern: Lower-class adolescents were more likely to say that they did not want to be rich, and references to work as a source of mobility were more common for lower-class subjects than for other classes.

Conclusion

Most of the analyses indicated that significant effects were largely age-related. Given the large number of analyses conducted, it may appear surprising that so few class or race effects emerged. Two conclusions may be tentatively warranted: First, class concepts are largely determined by cognitive level; second, functionalist influences toward greater legitimization of social inequality are relatively stronger than the influence of class consciousness.

There are some data in support of conflict theory—for example, greater concern by blacks or lower-class subjects for the consequences to the poor and greater willingness to challenge the economic structure. However, one must also note that for almost all analyses there were similar age trends and that most of these age trends were in favor of greater legitimization of inequality.

The increasing emphasis on equity concepts in explaining and justifying inequality is consistent with other studies of person perception (Livesley and Bromley, 1973) and the development of concepts of intelligence (Leahy and Hunt, 1983). By the age of ten the child has come to view different strata not only in terms of their different possessions or behavior, but also in terms of being different people. Of course, once the child views them as different people it becomes easier for him or her to justify a distributive justice system for extremes of wealth and poverty.

In our study of concepts of intellectual difference (Leahy and Hunt, 1983) we found that three levels of conception could be distinguished (see Exhibit 2). We refer to these levels as peripheral-obedient, psychological, and social interaction conceptions. As Exhibit 2 indicates, there is a shift from emphasis on concrete, peripheral behavior to a recognition of inferred psychological qualities to a recognition of the importance of the

Exhibit 2. Conceptions of Individual Differences in Intelligence

Level I: Peripheral-Obedient Conceptions
Intelligence is defined by actions, reading, knowledge of specific acts, and obedience to adult authority. Causes and changes in intelligence are conceptualized by passive obedience to adult authority or attendance at school. The view at this level is that the school should punish children who are not smart. Children deny the similarity of intelligent and unintelligent people.

Level II: Psychological Conceptions
Intelligence is defined by performance on tests, with an increased awareness that the intelligent and unintelligent groups are similar in that both are people and both can learn. Differences are attributed to motivation, studying, and training. Moral evaluations emerge, focusing on the lack of motivation presumed to characterize the unintelligent. Emphasis is on special tutoring and classes for the unintelligent.

Level III: Social Interaction Conceptions
There is emphasis on specific intellectual abilities associated with different kinds of intelligence. Intelligence is viewed as involving social competence, with groups of intelligent and unintelligent people seen as differing in personality traits. Differences in intelligence are attributed to social conformity and self-direction. Changes in intelligence are seen as resulting from psychological or motivational support and association with others.

social context of intelligence. These trends are similar to those described in Exhibit 1, in which levels of class concepts are shown. Concepts of social inequality undergo considerable qualitative change with age—resulting in the view that different strata are occupied by different *kinds* of people, not simply people with different possessions or different behavior.

I have proposed that cognitive development often carries costs, such that increasing development is associated with increasing capacity to engage in self-criticism and inequitable social comparison (Leahy, 1983c, 1985). The data on conceptions of social inequality—and the similar age trends irrespective of class or race—suggest that along with the stabilizing social effects of consensus, development also results in more stable dimensions (such as personality and worthiness) on which to judge the self or others. These "equity" explanations of inequality have the consequence of assuring a belief in a just world where the "losers" are viewed as obtaining their just due. Thus the unemployed—or, in the extreme, the homeless who have been displaced—would be viewed as failing to make it in a just world rather than being viewed as the innocent victims of market and labor policies.

References

Clark, K. B., and Clark, M. P. "Racial Identification and Preference in Negro Children." In T. M. Newcomb and E. L. Hartley (eds.), *Readings in Social Psychology*. New York: Holt, 1947.

Coie, J. D., and Pennington, B. F. "Children's Perception of Deviance and Disorder." *Child Development*, 1976, *47*, 407-413.

Elkind, D. "Egocentrism in Adolescence." *Child Development*, 1967, *38*, 1025-1034.

Feffer, M. "A Developmental Analysis of Interpersonal Behavior." *Psychological Review*, 1970, *77*, 197-214.

Hook, J. G. "The Development of Equity and Altruism in Judgments of Positive and Negative Justice." *Developmental Psychology*, 1982, *18*, 825-834.

Hook, J. G. "The Development of Children's Equity Judgments." In R. L. Leahy (ed.), *The Child's Construction of Social Inequality*. New York: Academic Press, 1983.

Inhelder, B., and Piaget, J. *The Growth of Logical Thinking from Childhood to Adolescence*. New York: Basic Books, 1958.

Kohlberg, L. "Stage and Sequence: The Cognitive-Developmental Approach to Socialization." In D. A. Goslin (ed.), *Handbook of Socialization: Theory and Research*. Skokie, Ill.: Rand McNally, 1969.

Lane, I., and Coon, R. "Reward Allocation in Preschool Children." *Child Development*, 1972, *43*, 1382-1389.

Leahy, R. L. "The Development of the Conception of Economic Incquality: I. Descriptions and Comparisons of Rich and Poor People." *Child Development*, 1981, *52*, 523-532.

Leahy, R. L. "The Development of the Conception of Economic Inequality: II. Explanations, Justifications, and Conceptions of Social Mobility and Social Change." *Developmental Psychology*, 1983a, *19*, 111-125.

Leahy, R. L. "The Development of the Conception of Economic Class." In R. L. Leahy (ed.), *The Child's Construction of Social Inequality*. New York: Academic Press, 1983b.

Leahy, R. L. "Development of Self and the Problems of Social Cognition: Identity Formation and Depression." In L. Wheeler and P. Shaver (eds.), *Review of Personality and Social Psychology*. Newbury Park, Calif.: Sage, 1983c.

Leahy, R. L. "The Costs of Development: Clinical Implications." In R. L. Leahy (ed.), *The Development of the Self*. New York: Academic Press, 1985.

Leahy, R. L. "Scripts and Cognitive Therapy: The Systemic Perspective." *Journal of Cognitive Psychotherapy*, in press.

Leahy, R. L., and Bresler, J. "Judgments of Sex-Role Traits: Masculinity-Femininity or Age Maturity?" Paper presented at meetings of the Eastern Psychological Association, Baltimore, 1982.

Leahy, R. L., and Hunt, T. "A Cognitive-Developmental Approach to the Development of Conceptions of Intelligence." In R. L. Leahy (ed.), *The Child's Construction of Social Inequality*. New York: Academic Press, 1983.

Leahy, R. L., and Shirk, S. "The Development of Classificatory Skills and Sex-Trait Stereotypes." *Sex Roles*, 1984, *10*, 281-292.

Lerner, M. "The Justice Motive: 'Equity' and 'Parity' Among Children." *Journal of Personality and Social Personality*, 1974, *29*, 539-550.

Leventhal, G., and Lane, D. "Sex, Age and Equity Behavior." *Journal of Personality and Social Personality*, 1970, *15*, 312-316.

Livesley, W., and Bromley, D. *Person Perception in Childhood and Adolescence*. New York: Wiley, 1973.

Marx, K. "Economic and Philosophical Manuscripts." In E. Fromm (ed.), *Marx's Concept of Man*. New York: Ungar, 1966. (Originally published 1844.)

Merton, R. *Social Theory and Social Structure*. New York: Free Press, 1957.

Paget, K. F. "Conceptions of Deviance and Disorder." In R. L. Leahy (ed.), *The Child's Construction of Social Inequality*. New York: Academic Press, 1983.

Parsons, T. *The Social System*. New York: Free Press, 1960.

Piaget, J. *The Language and Thought of the Child*. New York: Norton, 1926.

Piaget, J. *The Moral Judgment of the Child*. New York: Free Press, 1965. (Originally published 1932.)

Piaget, J. *Genetic Epistemology*. New York: Columbia University Press, 1970a.

Piaget, J. *Structuralism*. New York: Basic Books, 1970b.

Selman, R. *The Growth of Interpersonal Understanding*. New York: Academic Press, 1980.

Turiel, E. "Social Regulations and Domains of Social Concepts." In W. Damon (ed.), *Moral Development*. New Directions for Child Development, no. 2. San Francisco: Jossey-Bass, 1978.

Weber, M. *Essays in Sociology*. (H. Gerth and W. Mills, trans.) Oxford, England: Oxford University Press, 1946.

Williams, J., Bennett, S., and Best, D. "Awareness and Expression of Sex Stereotypes in Young Children." *Developmental Psychology*, 1975, *11*, 635-642.

Robert L. Leahy received his Ph.D. from Yale University. He is the director of the Center for Cognitive Therapy in New York City.

Name Index

Aber, M. S., 55, 67
Adams, A. V., 88, 95, 101
Adelson, J., 17, 18, 25
Albrecht, H. T., 3, 27, 47
Allen, V. L., 94, 95, 99, 101, 104
Allen, W. R., 90, 102, 103
Anderson, B., 88, 102
Anderson, R. N., 29, 44, 72, 86
Angell, R. C., 28, 44
Atwater, E., 87, 102

Baker, P., 4, 5
Bakke, E. W., 29, 44
Baldwin, J., 98, 102
Baltes, P. B., 95, 102
Bandura, A., 53, 66, 98, 102
Barbarin, O., 76, 84
Barnett, R. C., 94, 99, 102
Baruch, G. K., 94, 99, 102
Beale, R. L., 91, 103
Beiner, L., 94, 99, 102
Belle, D., 52, 67
Bennett, S., 109, 120
Bentler, P. M., 41, 44
Berndt, T., 54, 66
Berry, M. F., 98, 102
Best, D., 109, 120
Billings, A., 73, 84
Billingsley, A., 98, 102
Bjorck, J., 73, 84
Blair, K., 72, 84
Blassingame, J. W., 98, 102
Bluestone, B., 7, 25
Blundall, J., 72, 73, 85
Blyth, D. A., 33, 44
Bokemeier, J., 72, 84
Bonett, D. G., 41, 44
Bowman, P. J., 3, 87, 88, 89, 90, 91, 94, 95, 96, 97, 98, 99, 102, 103, 104, 105
Boykin, A. W., 95, 96, 102
Braithwaite, V. A., 33, 44
Braver, 57
Brenner, A., 53, 66
Bresler, J., 107, 120
Breur, H., 28, 44
Brim, O. G., 95, 102
Bromet, E. J., 7, 25

Bromley, D., 109, 118, 120
Bronfenbrenner, U., 9, 12, 21, 24
Burt, C., 73, 84
Buss, A. H., 36, 45
Buss, T., 50, 66

Carlton-Ford, S., 33, 44
Caspi, A., 10, 17, 19, 25, 29, 33, 39, 44, 50, 51, 65, 67
Cauce, A. M., 54, 55, 66, 67
Cavan, R. C., 28, 44
Cazenave, N. A., 91, 103
Center for the Study of Social Policy, 2, 5
Chesler, M., 76, 84
Children's Defense Fund, 1, 5
Churchill, H., 96, 104
Clark, K. B., 107, 119
Clark, M. P., 107, 119
Clark-Lempers, D., 8, 21, 25, 50, 51, 67, 73, 74, 83, 84, 85
Cochran, C., 72, 84
Cochran, M., 55, 68
Cohen, J., 31, 44, 73, 74, 84
Cohen, L., 73, 84
Cohen, P., 31, 44
Cohen, S., 94, 103
Cohn, J., 52, 66
Cohn, R., 12, 25
Coie, J. D., 109, 111, 119
Compas, B., 73, 84
Conger, R., 50, 53, 54, 63, 64, 66, 67, 73, 84
Coon, R., 112, 119
Cooper, J. E., 33, 44
Coopersmith, S., 51, 52, 66
Coyne, J., 52, 66
Cross, C. E., 29, 33, 45, 51, 67
Cunningham, S., 53, 66

D'Amico, R., 4, 5
D'Arcy, C., 73, 76, 84
Darrow, C. N., 104
DeBarsyshe, B., 52, 68
Dew, M. A., 7, 25
Doherty, M., 73, 85
Douvan, E., 17, 18, 25
Downey, G., 29, 33, 44, 52, 66

121

Dressler, W., 63, 66
DuBois, W.E.B., 98, 103
Duncan, G., 1, 2, 5
Duval, S., 39, 44
Duvall, E., 90, 103

Eccles, J. S., 7, 8, 25
Edelman, M. W., 2, 5
Elder, G. H., 2, 8, 10, 15, 17, 18, 21, 25, 26, 28, 29, 33, 36, 39, 44, 45, 50, 51, 52, 53, 54, 63, 64, 65, 66, 67, 82, 84
Elkind, D., 111, 119
Ensminger, M. E., 50, 67
Epps, E., 98, 103
Epstein, J. L., 17, 25
Erb, G., 72, 84
Erikson, E. H., 88, 95, 96, 99, 103
Etchison, D., 74, 85

Faber, S. S., 94, 103
Farley, R., 90, 102, 103
Farmer, V., 72, 85
Featherman, D. L., 12, 25
Feffer, M., 110, 111, 119
Felner, R. D., 54, 55, 66, 67, 94, 103
Feningstein, A., 36, 45
Flanagan, C. A., 2, 5, 6, 7, 15, 18, 21, 23, 25, 26, 51, 67
Florke, B., 73, 85
Foster, E., 53, 54, 63, 64, 67
Fox, G. L., 21, 25, 53, 67
Freeman, R. B., 88, 103

Galambos, N. L., 34, 45, 51, 67
Garfinkel, I., 52, 67
Garfinkle, B., 74, 85
Garkovitch, L., 72, 84
Gary, L. E., 94, 103
Gecas, V., 52, 67
George, L. K., 95, 99, 103
Gibbs, J., 50, 67
Gibson, R., 96, 103
Ginter, M., 54, 67
Goff, J., 67
Goldberg, D., 76, 85
Goode, W. J., 94, 99, 103
Green, B., 72, 85
Greene, E., 67
Gurin, G., 89, 90, 98, 102, 103, 104
Gurin, P., 98, 103
Guttentag, M., 52, 67

Halpen, R., 1, 5
Halton, L., 72, 85
Harding, V., 98, 103
Harold, R., 8, 25
Harrison, A. O., 91, 103
Harrison, B., 7, 25
Hartup, W., 73, 83, 86
Hatchett, D., 90, 103
Hatchett, S. J., 89, 90, 102
Hauser, R. M., 12, 25
Hauser, S., 52, 68
Heffernan, J., 72, 73, 85
Heffernan, W., 72, 73, 85
Heinelt, H., 28, 45
Herskovits, M. J., 98, 103
Herson, J., 67
Hetzer, H., 27, 45
Hill, R., 98, 103
Hiller, V. F., 76, 85
Hines, F., 72, 85
Hirsch, B. J., 55, 66, 67
Hoberman, H., 74, 85
Hoge, D. R., 33, 45
Holman, J., 33, 44
Hook, J. G., 112, 119
House, J. S., 7, 17, 21, 22, 25
Howard, D. S., 95, 98, 102
Hughes, D., 76, 84
Hunt, T., 107, 109, 115, 118, 120

Inhelder, B., 112, 119
Isralowitz, R., 51, 67

Jackson, J. S., 89, 90, 96, 98, 102, 103, 104
Jahoda, M., 28, 39, 45
Jameson, J., 67
Johnson, J., 55, 68
Jolly, B., 72, 85
Jones, R. L., 88, 94, 95, 96, 103
Jöreskog, K. G., 36, 37, 45

Kahn, R. L., 94, 99, 103
Kain, E. L., 8, 15, 21, 26
Kaplan, H. B., 33, 34, 45
Keating, N., 73, 85
Kedar-Voivodas, G., 17, 25
Kellam, S., 50, 67
Kelley, R., 53, 67
Kelly, R., 21, 25
Keniston, D., 87, 104
Kenkel, M., 73, 85

Name Index

Kessler, R. C., 7, 17, 21, 22, 25, 33, 45, 94, 104
Kilman, S., 74, 85
Kilner, L., 52, 68
Kinder, D. R., 96, 104
King, L., 50, 68
Kjenaas, M., 73, 85
Klein, E. B., 104
Knaub, P., 72, 85
Kohlberg, L., 108, 110, 111, 119
Kornblum, W., 54, 68
Kropp, J., 66, 84

Lahey, B., 66, 84
Lane, D., 112, 120
Lane, I., 112, 119
Langner, R., 50, 67
Larson, J. H., 29, 45
Lazarfeld, P. F., 28, 39, 45
Leahy, R. L., 4, 107, 108, 109, 110, 112, 115, 118, 119, 120
Lee, P. C., 17, 25
Lempers, J., 50, 51, 67, 73, 74, 85
Lempers, R., 8, 21, 25
Lerner, M., 112, 120
Leventhal, G., 112, 120
Levinson, D. F., 87, 95, 99, 104
Levinson, M. H., 104
Levinson, P., 50, 67
Lieberman, M. A., 94, 104
Liebow, E., 91, 96, 104
Liem, J. H., 7, 17, 21, 25, 33, 45, 49, 68
Liem, R., 7, 17, 21, 25, 33, 45, 49, 68
Liker, J. K., 29, 33, 45, 51, 67
Little, L., 72, 85
Lively, W., 109, 118, 120
Longfellow, C., 50, 52, 68

McCarty, J. D., 33, 45, 66, 84
McCullough, W., 98, 103
McGranahan, D., 72, 86
McKee, B., 104
McLanahan, S., 52, 67
McLoyd, V. C., 3, 5, 6, 22, 25, 49, 52, 65, 68, 69
McPartland, J. M., 17, 25
Makosky, V. P., 50, 63, 68
Malveaux, J., 88, 95, 104
Mangum, G. L., 88, 95, 101
Marlow, J., 72, 85
Marsiglio, W., 91, 104

Martin, E. P., 98, 104
Martin, J. M., 98, 104
Marx, K., 108, 110, 116, 120
Menaghan, E. G., 94, 104
Merton, R. K., 94, 95, 99, 104, 107, 108, 120
Miller, P., 54, 68
Moen, P., 8, 15, 21, 25
Moos, R. H., 29, 45, 73, 84, 94, 104
Morris, A., 98, 104
Mullan, S., 94, 104
Munro, B., 73, 85
Myers, H. F., 50, 68

NASW News, 72, 73, 86
National Action Commission on the Mental Health of Rural America, 73, 85
Neighbors, H. W., 98, 104
Netusil, A., 73, 74, 83, 84
Nobles, W., 98, 104
Norem, R., 72, 73, 85
Nunally, J. C., 31, 45

Office of Technology Assessment, 72, 85
Ogbu, J., 96, 104
Ondeck, C., 89, 104

Paget, K. F., 109, 111, 120
Parson, J., 74, 85
Parsons, T., 107, 108, 116, 120
Patterson, G., 52, 68
Pearlin, L. I., 76, 86, 94, 95, 99, 104
Pennington, B. F., 109, 111, 119
Perkins, J., 72, 86
Petrulis, M., 72, 85
Piaget, J., 108, 111, 112, 119, 120
Policy Forum on Rural Stress, 73, 86
Poole, M., 74, 86
Powers, S., 52, 68
Price, R. H., 94, 104
Primavera, J., 54, 55, 66, 67, 94, 103
Prouix, F., 72, 85

Quinn, R. P., 103

Radin, N., 8, 25
Ramsey, E., 52, 68
Ranch, K. H., 28, 44
Redburn, F. S., 50, 66
Reischl, T., 55, 66, 67

Reiss, D., 73, 86
Reitzler, M., 34, 37, 45
Ricchiardi, S., 72, 86
Riley, D., 55, 68
Riley, N., 90, 104
Rodgers, W., 2, 5
Rodgers-Rose, L. F., 94, 104
Rollins, B., 52, 68
Rosen, E., 53, 63, 68
Rosenblatt, P., 72, 73, 86
Rosenthal, R. A., 103
Ross, H. L., 22, 26
Rostkowski, J., 67

Salamon, S., 72, 86
Salasin, S., 52, 67
Sandler, I., 54, 57, 66, 68
Sarbin, T. R., 94, 95, 99, 104
Saunders, E., 50, 52, 68
Sawhill, I., 88, 102
Sawhill, L. Y., 22, 26
Scarr, S., 28, 45
Scheier, M. F., 36, 44, 45
Schindler, H., 33, 36, 45
Schooler, C., 76, 86, 95, 104
Schoor-Theisen, I., 28, 44
Schulberg, H. C., 7, 25
Selman, R., 110, 120
Sheets, C., 96, 104
Sheldon, A., 21, 25, 53, 67
Sherrod, L. R., 28, 46
Shirk, S., 107, 112, 115, 120
Short, J., 54, 68
Siddique, C. M., 73, 76, 84
Silbereisen, R. K., 3, 27, 28, 34, 37, 44, 45, 46, 47, 51, 67
Silverberg, S. B., 17, 18, 26, 39, 46
Simmons, R. G., 33, 44
Simons, R. L., 8, 21, 25, 50, 51, 67, 73, 74, 85
Singer, M., 51, 67
Slavin, L., 84
Smets, A., 73, 83, 86
Smith, R., 51, 54, 68
Snoek, J. D., 103
Sörbom, D., 36, 37, 45
Sproat, K. V., 96, 104
Staples, R., 94, 105
Statistisches Bundesamt, 28, 46
Statuto, C. S., 17, 25
Steinberg, L. D., 17, 18, 26, 39, 46
Stevenson-Long, J., 95, 105

Sudarkasa, N., 98, 105
Sundberg, N., 74, 86

Thomas, D., 52, 68
Toms, F. D., 95, 102
Treadwell, M., 55, 68
Trent, W. T., 90, 105
Troll, L. W., 90, 105
Tronick, E., 52, 66
Turiel, E., 112, 120
Turner, J. B., 7, 17, 21, 22, 25
Turner, R., 50, 67
Tyler, L., 74, 86

United Community Services, 15, 26
U.S. Department of Commerce, 10, 26

Van Hook, M. P., 3, 71, 73
Van Hoose, W. H., 95, 105
Van Nguyen, T., 18, 25, 29, 33, 39, 44, 50, 51, 65, 67
Vande Vliert, E., 94, 99, 101
Vannatta, K., 73, 84
Verdonik, F., 28, 46

Wacker, A., 28, 45
Wagner, B., 73, 84
Walker, J., 73, 74, 82, 85
Walper, S., 3, 27, 30, 31, 34, 37, 46, 47
Walper, W., 46
Walsh, F., 73, 86
Weber, M., 108, 110, 116, 120
Weiss, R. S., 19, 26, 64, 65, 68
Welzer, H., 28, 45
Werner, E., 51, 54, 68
Wetzels, P., 33, 36, 45
Wicklund, R. A., 39, 44
Wiegal, R., 86
Wilkening, E., 72, 86
William T. Grant Foundation Commission on Work, Family, and Citizenship, 55, 68
Williams, J., 96, 105, 109, 120
Williams, T., 54, 68
Wills, T. A., 94, 103
Wilson, L., 3, 49, 69
Wilson, W. J., 2, 5, 88, 96, 105
Wise, D. A., 88, 103
Wolchik, S., 54, 57, 68
Wolfe, D. M., 103
Wool, H., 89, 105
Worth, M. R., 95, 105

Wortman, C. B., 94, 104
Wright, S., 73, 86

Yang, R., 66, 84

Zank, S., 34, 37, 45, 46
Zeisel, H., 28, 39, 45
Zelkowitz, P., 50, 52, 68
Zykorie, D., 67

Subject Index

Achievement models, parents' role as, 3, 8, 12-14,
Adolescent autonomy, 17-19
Adolescent-to-adult transition, in black youth, 87-88
Affirmative action policies, 4, 101

Behavioral problems, in economically deprived children, 27-28, 51, 52, 73, 78.
Berlin Youth Longitudinal Study, 3, 27-28, 43-44; effects of income loss on family relationships (Study 1) in, 29-32; family as mediator of adolescent transgression (Study 2) in, 33-36; further evidence from longitudinal data (Study 4) in, 39-43; personal risk in coping with economic hardship (Study 3) in, 36-39
Birleson's Self-Rating Scale of Depression, 56
Black youth: approaches to chronic job search strain in, 94-98; and chronic joblessness, 3-4, 88-90, 99-101; cultural resources for, 4, 95, 98-101; and educational opportunities, 96, 100-101; and gender differences in job search strain, 91-94; and job search discouragement, 89-90, 99-101; and mental health during economic hardship, 63; and modes of coping, 97-98, 100; and poverty, 2; and support systems, 54

Center for Epidemiological Studies Depression Scale (CES-D), 57
Change in Parents' Work Lives and Adolescent Adjustment study, 8
Child-rearing behavior, 3, 12, 50
Children's Inventory of Social Support, 57
Children's Manifest Anxiety Scale, 56
Class-concept study, 113-116
Class consciousness, 110, 117
Cognitive-developmental stratification theory, 108-109, 114, 116, 117; and decentration, 110-111; and distributive justice, 111-112; natural ordering of concepts in, 109-110
Communication patterns: of rural families, 74, 78-79, 82; of single mothers, 3, 49, 57, 59, 61, 64
Conflict stratification theory, 108, 114-117
Coping strategies: of black youth, 97-98, 100; in the Great Depression, 29; of rural adolescents, 76, 80-82; of single mothers, 53-54, 57, 61, 63-64
Cultural resources, for black youth, 4, 95, 98-101

Decentration, 110-111
Decision-making processes, 3, 16-19
Demotions, 11, 13, 14, 28
Drug use, in rural adolescents, 51, 73

Economic change: designing prospective developmental studies in, 23-24; and early adolescents' development, 21; and effect on families, 9, 16-19; methodological issues in, 21-24; objective measures of, 21; and parent-adolescent decision making, 16-19; and quality of parent-adolescent authority relationships, 19; subjective measures of, 21-22
Economic hardship: adolescents' perceptions of, 21; and child development, 7-9, 28-29, 50-54, 56, 60; and impact on families, 73-74; long-term consequences of, 15, 82; maternal behavior during, 51, 57-61, 65; and parental mental health, 49-50, 58-59, 63-66; personal risk in coping with, 36-39
Economic inequality, 1, 4, 107-108, 115-117. *See also* Social stratification systems Economic recession. *See* Recession
Education: changes in adolescents' aspirations for, 12-15; effects of recession on, 2, 3, 9, 19-20; income loss and parental levels of, 34-36;

of parents in a work status change, 11-12

Families, and recession, 2-3, 7-12, 21-24. *See also* Transitions in Early Adolescence Study
Family cohesion, 76, 80
Family composition events, and economic decline, 1
Family Decision-Making Scale, 17
Family flexibility, 76, 80-82
Family integration: effect of parental strains on, 3, 27, 29-32; and level of parental education, 34-36; and sensitivity to evaluation by significant others, 36-38; and sensitivity to peer evaluation, 39-43; and transgression proneness, 33-34
Family relationships, effects of income loss on, 29-32, 43
Family system, changes in, 28, 77, 81
Farm crisis, 3, 71-73; and adolescent career plans, 81; adolescent perceptions of, 77-81; and coping efforts, 76, 80-82; and family and community information networks, 78-79, 82; impact on families and adolescents, 73-74; study of rural adolescents in, 74-76
Female-headed households. *See* Single mothers
Functional stratification theory, 108, 115, 116

Gender differences: in job search strain, 91-94; in parent-adolescent authority relationships, 17, 18
General Health Questionnaire, 75-76, 78
Great Depression, studies on impact of, 2, 15, 19, 24, 28, 29, 39, 51, 82

Hopkins Symptom Checklist, 57

Income loss, 3; and adolescents' problem behavior, 27-28; and effects on family relationships, 29-32. *See also* Berlin Youth Longitudinal Study
Intelligence difference conceptions, in social inequality, 117-118
Iowa farm crisis study, 74-81. *See also* Farm crisis

Job search strain, 4, 88; and gender differences, 90-94; life cycle approach to, 3, 94-100
Joblessness, 3-4, 88-89; and discouragement, 89-90, 99-101
Juvenile delinquency, in rural youth, 51, 73. *See also* Behavioral problems

Labor market events, and economic decline, 1
Layoffs, 8, 10, 11, 13-15, 17
Life chances, 110
Likert scales, 13
LISREL multiple group comparison approach, 36, 37, 40

Maternal behavior, during economic hardship, 51, 57-61, 65
Maternal decision-making power, 3, 30-32
Maternal responses, to change in family work status, 16, 28
Mental health. *See* Psychological well-being

National Longitudinal Survey of Youth Labor Market Experience, 4
Negative life events, and children's psychological well-being, 58, 60, 62

Occupational aspirations, of adolescents, 12-15
Organizational unity, 109, 110

Panel Study of Income Dynamics (PSID), 1, 2
Parent-adolescent authority relations, 3, 7-9, 16-19, 29
Parental discipline, during economic hardships, 51, 57
Parental reaction, to unemployment, 53
Peer relationships, sensitivity to, 39-43
Personality development studies. *See* Berlin Youth Longitudinal Study
Poverty, 1, 2, 4, 21, 52
Psychological well-being of children, 3, 50-54, 56, 63-66; and demographic factors, 60, 62-63; and economic factors, 62-63; impact of maternal behavior on, 58-61, 65;

multivariate model of, 60-63; and negative life events, 60; and social support, 60, 62
Psychological well-being of parents, and effects on children, 3, 49-50, 52-54, 57-59, 63-65

Recession, and the effects on families and schools, 2-3, 7-12, 19-24. See also Transitions in Early Adolescence Study
Reemployment, compensatory effects of, 3, 17
Responsibility, burden of, on rural youth, 79-80, 82
Role-strain adaptation processes, 94-97, 99
Rural adolescents, 3, 51. See also Farm crisis

School-to-work transition, for black youth, 87-88
Schools, effects of recession on, 2, 3, 9, 19-20
Self-derogation: and level of parental education, 34-36; and sensitivity to evaluation by significant others, 36-38; and sensitivity to peer evaluation, 39-43; and transgression proneness, 33-34
Self-esteem, in economically deprived children, 3, 27, 51, 52, 66. See also Self-derogation
Sensitivity: to evaluations by significant others, 36-41; to peer evaluations, 39-43
Single mothers, 2, 3, 51-53, 63-66; study of, 56-63
Social change, concepts of, 117
Social inequality, concepts of, 108, 118-119. See also Social stratification systems
Social stratification systems, 107-108; age trends in, 117; and class-concepts study, 113-116; cognitive-development model of, 109-112; models of, 108-109; and sociocentric thinking, 110; and systemic thinking, 110
Socialization processes, 2, 12-15, 74
Socioeconomic status, and change in work status, 11-12
Socioemotional functioning. See Psychological well-being.
Standard of living, decline in, 1, 7
Stressful Life Events Inventory for Children, 58
Structural isomorphism, in the cognitive-development stratification model, 110
Suicide attempts, in rural adolescents, 82, 83
Support networks, 54-58, 60-62, 65

Transgression proneness, 51; effects of family integration and adolescent self-derogation on, 33-34; and level of parental education, 34-36; and sensitivity to evaluation by significant others, 36-38; and sensitivity to peer evaluations, 39-43
Transitions in Early Adolescence Study, 2-3, 7-12, 21-24; economic change and parent-adolescent decision making (Study 2) in, 16-19; effects of the recession on schools (Study 3) in, 19-21; parental work status and the socialization of adolescents' aspirations (Study 1) in, 12-15

Unemployment, 1-4, 7, 12, 20-22, 24, 28, 53

Work status change, 3, 10-12; and achievement socialization processes, 9, 12-15; and adolescent adjustment, 8, 9; and adolescents' satisfaction with family decision making, 18; maternal response to, 16, 28; and parent-adolescent authority relationships, 16; during recessionary periods, 21-24. See also Transitions in Early Adolescence Study

Ordering Information

NEW DIRECTIONS FOR CHILD DEVELOPMENT is a series of paperback books that presents the latest research findings on all aspects of children's psychological development, including their cognitive, social, moral, and emotional growth. Books in the series are published quarterly, in Fall, Winter, Spring, and Summer, and are available for purchase by subscription as well as by single copy.

SUBSCRIPTIONS for 1989-90 cost $48.00 for individuals (a savings of 20 percent over single-copy prices) and $64.00 for institutions, agencies, and libraries. Please do not send institutional checks for personal subscriptions. Standing orders are accepted.

SINGLE COPIES cost $14.95 when payment accompanies order. (California, New Jersey, New York, and Washington, D.C., residents please include appropriate sales tax.) Billed orders will be charged postage and handling.

DISCOUNTS FOR QUANTITY ORDERS are available. Please write to the address below for information.

ALL ORDERS must include either the name of an individual or an official purchase order number. Please submit your order as follows:
Subscriptions: specify series and year subscription is to begin
Single copies: include individual title code (such as CD1)

MAIL ALL ORDERS TO:
Jossey-Bass Inc., Publishers
350 Sansome Street
San Francisco, California 94104

OTHER TITLES AVAILABLE IN THE
NEW DIRECTIONS FOR CHILD DEVELOPMENT SERIES
William Damon, Editor-in-Chief

CD45 Infant Stress and Coping, *Michael Lewis, John Worobey*
CD44 Empathy and Related Emotional Responses, *Nancy Eisenberg*
CD43 Maternal Responsiveness: Characteristics and Consequences, *Marc H. Bornstein*
CD42 Black Children and Poverty: A Developmental Perspective, *Diana T. Slaughter*
CD41 Children's Mathematics, *Geoffrey B. Saxe, Maryl Gearhart*
CD40 Parental Behavior in Diverse Societies, *Robert A. LeVine, Patrice M. Miller, Mary Maxwell West*
CD39 Developmental Psychopathology and Its Treatment, *Ellen D. Nannis, Philip A. Cowan*
CD38 Children's Gender Schemata, *Lynn S. Liben, Margaret L. Signorella*
CD37 Adolescent Social Behavior and Health, *Charles E. Irwin, Jr.*
CD36 Symbolic Development in Atypical Children, *Dante Cicchetti, Marjorie Beeghly*
CD35 How Children and Adolescents View the World of Work, *John H. Lewko*
CD34 Maternal Depression and Infant Disturbance, *Edward Z. Tronick, Tiffany Field*
CD33 Children's Intellectual Rights, *David Moshman*
CD32 Early Experience and the Development of Competence, *William Fowler*
CD31 Temperament and Social Interaction in Infants and Children, *Jacqueline V. Lerner, Richard M. Lerner*
CD30 Identity in Adolescence: Processes and Contents, *Alan S. Waterman*
CD29 Peer Conflict and Psychological Growth, *Marvin W. Berkowitz*
CD28 Children and Computers, *Elisa L. Klein*
CD27 The Development of Reading Skills, *Thomas H. Carr*
CD26 Childhood Depression, *Dante Cicchetti, Karen Schneider-Rosen*
CD25 Analyzing Children's Play Dialogues, *Frank Kessel, Artin Göncü*
CD24 Children in Families Under Stress, *Anna-Beth Doyle, Dolores Gold, Debbie S. Moscowitz*
CD23 Children's Learning in the "Zone of Proximal Development," *Barbara Rogoff, James V. Wertsch*
CD22 Adolescent Development in the Family, *Harold D. Grotevant, Catherine R. Cooper*
CD21 Levels and Transitions in Children's Development, *Kurt W. Fischer*
CD20 Child Development and International Development: Research-Policy Interfaces, *Daniel A. Wagner*
CD19 Children and Divorce, *Lawrence A. Kurdek*
CD18 Children's Planning Strategies, *David Forbes, Mark T. Greenberg*
CD17 Developmental Approaches to Giftedness and Creativity, *David Henry Feldman*
CD16 Emotional Development, *Dante Cicchetti, Petra Hesse*
CD15 Children's Conceptions of Spatial Relationships, *Robert Cohen*
CD14 Children's Conceptions of Health, Illness, and Bodily Functions, *Roger Bibace, Mary E. Walsh*

CD13 Viewing Children Through Television, *Hope Kelly, Howard Gardner*
CD12 Cognitive Development, *Kurt W. Fischer*
CD11 Developmental Perspectives on Child Maltreatment, *Ross Rizley, Dante Cicchetti*
CD10 Children's Memory, *Marion Perlmutter*
CD9   Children's Play, *Kenneth H. Rubin*
CD8   Anthropological Perspectives on Child Development, *Charles M. Super, Sara Harkness*
CD7   Clinical-Developmental Psychology, *Robert L. Selman, Regina Yando*
CD6   Fact, Fiction, and Fantasy in Childhood, *Ellen Winner, Howard Gardner*
CD5   Intellectual Development Beyond Childhood, *Deanna Kuhn*
CD4   Social Interaction and Communication During Infancy, *Ina C. Uzgiris*
CD2   Moral Development, *William Damon*
CD1   Social Cognition, *William Damon*

U.S. Postal Service
STATEMENT OF OWNERSHIP, MANAGEMENT AND CIRCULATION
Required by 39 U.S.C. 3685

1A. Title of Publication: New Directions for Child Development
1B. Publication No.: 494-090
2. Date of Filing: 10/27/89
3. Frequency of Issue: quarterly
3A. No. of Issues Published Annually: 4
3B. Annual Subscription Price: $48 individual / $64 institutional

4. Complete Mailing Address of Known Office of Publication: 350 Sansome Street, San Francisco, CA 94104-1310

5. Complete Mailing Address of the Headquarters of General Business Offices of the Publisher: (above address)

6. Full Names and Complete Mailing Address of Publisher, Editor, and Managing Editor

Publisher: Jossey-Bass Inc., Publishers (above address)

Editor: William Damon, Dept. of Education, Box 1938, Brown University, Providence, RI 02912

Managing Editor: Steven Piersanti, President, Jossey-Bass Inc., Publishers (above address)

7. Owner

Full Name	Complete Mailing Address
Maxwell Communications Corp. plc	Headington Hill Hall, Oxford OX30BW, U.K.

8. Known Bondholders, Mortgagees, and Other Security Holders Owning or Holding 1 Percent or More of Total Amount of Bonds, Mortgages or Other Securities

Full Name	Complete Mailing Address
none	

10. Extent and Nature of Circulation

	Average No. Copies Each Issue During Preceding 12 Months	Actual No. Copies of Single Issue Published Nearest to Filing Date
A. Total No. Copies (Net Press Run)	1300	1250
B. Paid and/or Requested Circulation		
1. Sales through dealers and carriers, street vendors and counter sales	208	76
2. Mail Subscription (Paid and/or requested)	523	522
C. Total Paid and/or Requested Circulation (Sum of 10B1 and 10B2)	731	598
D. Free Distribution by Mail, Carrier or Other Means Samples, Complimentary, and Other Free Copies	185	180
E. Total Distribution (Sum of C and D)	916	778
F. Copies Not Distributed		
1. Office use, left over, unaccounted, spoiled after printing	384	472
2. Return from News Agents		
G. TOTAL (Sum of E, F1 and 2—should equal net press run shown in A)	1300	1250

11. I certify that the statements made by me above are correct and complete

Signature and Title of Editor, Publisher, Business Manager, or Owner: Vice-President

PS Form 3526, Feb. 1989